# HITLER'S DECISION TO
# INVADE RUSSIA
## 1941

ROBERT CECIL

———

# Hitler's Decision to Invade Russia 1941

———

David McKay Company, Inc.
New York

# CONTENTS

What is the world, O soldiers?
    It is I;
I, this incessant snow;
    This northern sky;
Soldiers, this solitude
    Through which we go
    Is I

WALTER DE LA MARE: *Napoleon*


Wir ziehen hinaus in die Ferne
    Vom Dunkel der Nacht noch umloht;
Im Osten verblassen die Sterne,
    Vorwaerts ins Morgenrot!

(We'll take the distant trail
    That still in darkness lies;
In the East the stars grow pale,
    On, on to the sunrise!)

HITLER-JUGEND song

# EDITORS' INTRODUCTION

Numerous books and articles have been written about the weapons, battles and campaigns of the Second World War, and the problems of command, supply and intelligence have been extensively surveyed. Yet, though the fighting has been so fully described from these and other points of view, the reasons why the various military operations took place have attracted less study and remain comparatively obscure. It is to fill this gap in the understanding of the Second World War that this series has been conceived.

The perceptive have always understood the extent to which war is a continuation of policy by other means, and the clash of armies or fleets has, in intention, seldom been haphazard. Battles and campaigns often contain the keys to the understanding of the grand strategies of supreme commands and the political aims and purpose of nations and alliances.

In each of the volumes in this series an important battle or campaign is assessed from the point of view of discovering its relationship to the war as a whole, for in asking the questions Why was this battle fought? and What effect did it produce? one is raising the issue of the real meaning and character of the war.

As the series progresses, its readers, advancing case by case, will be able to make general judgements about the central character of the Second World War. Some will find this worthwhile in its own right; others will see it as a means of increasing their grasp of the contemporary scene. Thirty years have now passed since the death of Hitler and the capitulation of Japan. These momentous events were the culmination of a war which transformed the political and social, the economic and technological and, indeed, the general conditions of society and politics in virtually every corner of the world.

NOBLE FRANKLAND
CHRISTOPHER DOWLING

# ABBREVIATIONS

DBFP:  Documents on British Foreign Policy.
DGFP:  Documents on German Foreign Policy.

IMT:  International Military Tribunal.

KTB:  Kriegstagebuch (War Diary).

OKH:  Oberkommando der Heeres (Army High Command).

OKW:  Oberkommando der Wehrmacht (Commissariat Armed Forces High Command).

NKVD:  People's Commissariat for Internal Affairs.
NSDAP:  German National-Socialist Workers' Party.

SD:  Sicherheitsdienst (Security Service).
SS:  Schutzstaffeln (Secret Police).

VfZg:  Vierteljahreshefte fuer Zeitgeschichte (Quarterly of Contemporary History).

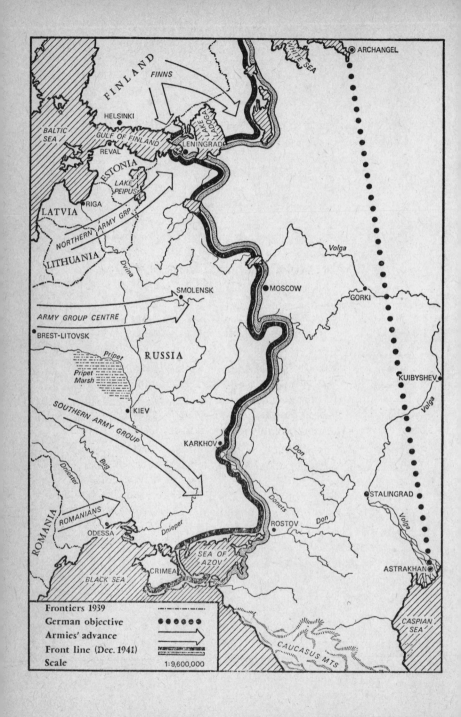

FINNS

FINLAND

HELSINKI

BALTIC SEA

GULF OF FINLAND

REVAL

ESTONIA

LAKE PEIPUS

LATVIA

RIGA

NORTHERN ARMY GRP

LITHUANIA

Dvina

LAKE LADOGA

LENINGRAD

WHITE SEA

ARCHANGEL

Volga

SMOLENSK

ARMY GROUP CENTRE

BREST-LITOVSK

Pripet

Pripet Marsh

RUSSIA

MOSCOW

GORKI

KUIBYSHEV

Volga

SOUTHERN ARMY GROUP

KIEV

KARKHOV

Don

Donets

Dnieper

Bug

Dniester

ROMANIA

ROMANIANS

ODESSA

CRIMEA

SEA OF AZOV

BLACK SEA

ROSTOV

Don

STALINGRAD

Volga

ASTRAKHAN

CASPIAN SEA

CAUCASUS MTS

| Frontiers 1939 | ----- |
| German objective | ●●●●●● |
| Armies' advance | → |
| Front line (Dec. 1941) | |
| Scale | 1:9,600,000 |

# I

## Teutons and Slavs

Joseph Goebbels ended his article in *Das Reich* of 6 July 1941 with the words: 'The command to advance issued by the Fuehrer during the night of 22 June was an act of world historical importance. It will probably pass into history as the decisive act of this war.'[1] For once the great deceiver spoke the truth. Indeed one authority has gone further and written: 'In the days when the history of the twentieth century can be written as a whole it may be found that one single event dominated it, namely Hitler's invasion of Russia.'[2] If this verdict is justified, there is no need to apologize for offering to the reading public another interpretation of the motivations and attendant circumstances that led to Hitler's decision.

Let us look briefly at this verdict before beginning to study the decision. First, Hitler's fatal error, coupled with his refusal even to examine the possibilities of a compromise peace with Stalin, ensured not only that Germany would lose the war, but that the Russians would be drawn into the heart of Europe in pursuit of the retreating forces of the Third Reich. Secondly, the extinction of German power and the subsequent partition of the country played at least as large a part as the defeat of France and the exhaustion of Britain in making certain that Europe would never again dominate world politics, as in the past. Thirdly, the elimination of Europe as an independent power factor, combined with the garrisoning of post-war Germany by the USA and USSR, contributed disastrously to the Cold War confrontation, aggravated by ideological differences, between the two super-powers. Hitler himself glimpsed this development earlier than most, when he wrote in his testament in February 1945: 'The laws of both history and geography

---

1 *Wollt Ihr den totalen Krieg?* W. A. Boelke (Munich, 1969), p.239
2 *The House Built on Sand:* G. Reitlinger (London, 1960), p.9

will compel these two powers to a trial of strength, either military or in the field of economics and ideology. These same laws make it inevitable that both these powers should become enemies of Europe.'[3] One does not have to be a disillusioned dictator in order to see that it is inimical to the interests of Europe, as a whole, to be divided between the spheres of two super-powers with interests extending far beyond the confines of the European continent.

VE-Day marked the end of another era – that of the centennial struggle between Teuton and Slav. This cannot be studied in depth in these pages, but some account of it is necessary to provide the backcloth against which Hitler's decision was enacted. We shall examine in the next chapter his racial and ideological prejudices and his megalomanic sense of the commingled destiny of himself and the Germanic peoples. That sense and those prejudices were not shared by all Germans, nor even by the whole of the NSDAP; but there prevailed in the Third Reich a climate of opinion that tolerated them, even where they were not altogether approved. One aspect of this lamentable tolerance touched upon the traditional attitude of Teutonic towards Slav peoples and helped to condition the minds of those who shared in planning the campaign and in fighting it with such ruthless savagery.

How else explain the belief of so many Germans, besides Hitler, that Russia, contrary to the lesson of history, would be so swiftly subdued in one brief campaign, for which inadequate preparation had been made? How else explain the failure of the Wehrmacht, which had fought an honourable campaign in the west, to offer any open remonstrance before the outbreak of the Russian war against relinquishing the rear areas, as it advanced, to the SS, well knowing from experience in Poland what the fate of the inhabitants would be? How else explain the complete failure of German military planners to make provision for the Russian prisoners of war who, in strict accordance with their expectations, fell into German

---

[3] *The Testament of A. Hitler:* ed. F. Genoud (London, 1961), p.107

hands in such vast numbers in the first stage of the war and died in captivity in such pitiable profusion? These and other questions cannot be answered solely in terms of Hitler's sadistic spirit and his dominance over the minds of those who served him. Ideas of racial superiority and historic destiny were not the exclusive property of Hitler and the NSDAP; they lay buried in the national consciousness, awaiting the demonic summons of Germany's Fuehrer. In that sense neither 1933 nor 1941 represented a break with the past.

Whilst we need not accept the dubious Nazi premise that racial factors determine a nation's history, we must concede at the outset that the movements of peoples in Central and Eastern Europe at various periods since the fifth century created ethnographic and demographic patterns that would have taxed the capacities of the most pacific peoples and the most enlightened statesmen. The early Slavs, who between the fifth and seventh centuries moved West to a line running roughly from the Elbe to the Adriatic, gave the appellation '*Niemcy*', or dumb, to the Teutonic tribes whom they encountered. One of these tribal groups, the Goths, gave to the Slav peoples their name by first calling them '*Slavan*', or silent.[4] It has ever since remained in large measure a *dialogue des sourds*.

It has sometimes been assumed that conflict between Teuton and Slav was sharpened by religious differences, and there is certainly truth in this view in relation to the colonization of the Baltic coastline by the Teutonic Knights, which was a favourite theme of Nazi mythology; but we cannot find in religion an explanation of the hostility between the Teutonic Knights and the Poles, since both parties were Roman Catholic. Further south the same was true of the West Slavs of Bohemia and Moravia and the neighbouring Bavarians, though in the Hussite Wars it was sometimes difficult to distinguish between racial antagonism and suppression of heresy. Later the Habsburgs brought the Counter-Reformation into Silesia

[4] *Teuton and Slav:* H. Schreiber (London, 1965), pp.40-1

13

at the expense of both Slav and German Protestants, without in the process bringing the two racial groups much closer together.

More relevant to our theme is the war of words between German and Slav archaeologists and historians about the origins of civilization and urbanization in Central and Eastern Europe. Western writers, including Germans, have usually underestimated the evidence that in the Middle Ages civilization advanced along the inland waterways linking the Black Sea to the Baltic in much the same way as it did along the salt-water littoral of Western Europe and the Mediterranean. Where evidence of urbanization in Slav lands was unmistakable, as in the kingdom of Kiev, it was ascribed not to the capability of indigenous Slavs, but to the Nordic influence of the Varangians – also 'heroes of culture' to the Nazis. As a corollary, it was further assumed that civilization had always moved from West to East and that its harbingers had been the Teutonic peoples, who were pushing out in that direction between the eleventh and fifteenth centuries. The final deduction was the firm belief that the Teutons were the great civilizing force, in contrast to the Slavs, who were a backward race, incapable, except under Teutonic leadership, of building cities, founding states or creating their own culture.

Once contempt for another race has become ingrained, it is easy to find supporting evidence for that contempt. The temptation to do so was particularly strong in the nineteenth century, when the industrial revolution, for reasons unconnected with race, scarcely penetrated east of a line from the Elbe to the Sudeten mountains, which approximately marked the end of the main concentrations of Germans. From this fact derived the conviction, surviving almost until the atomic age, that Slav peoples were technologically inept. German colonization did not follow a consistent pattern in all areas. Prussia had been conquered by the Teutonic Knights with fire and sword; this laid the foundations of the great *Junker* estates in sparsely populated country, where Slav labour continued to be needed. Further north and east more of the indigenous inhabitants survived and German settlement was largely confined to the land-owning 'Baltic Barons' and the trading population of cities such as Riga and Memel. Germanization and industrialization marched hand in hand in Silesia, after the conquest of the province by Frederick the Great; possibilities of amicable co-operation in this area between Teuton and Slav were fatally affected by the determination of the Hohenzollerns to link Silesia to East Prussia. At the end of the eighteenth century Prussia, Russia and Austria shared in successive partitions of Poland, which were confirmed by the general settlement of 1815.

From the time that Prussia began to emerge as a great power her relations with Russia partook of the nature of an anti-Polish conspiracy. Bismarck was further influenced to keep this friendship in good repair by the hostility of France and the need to avoid fighting on two fronts. At home, however, his policy was anti-Slav; his *Kulturkampf* was directed against Poles as Slavs as much as against Poles as Catholics. The Second Reich set up a German Settlement Commission in 1886 to buy up land for German farmers, who were obliged to take German wives; in 1908 the Commission was given power to expropriate Polish-owned property.[5] Two factors were beginning to sour German relations not only with Poles, but also with the more distant Russians. One was German fear of the higher Slav birth-rate. The Slavs were, as Hitler told Rauschning, 'an inferior race that breed like vermin';[6] to deprive them of land would reduce their fertility. This had become a part of German folklore long before the NSDAP came into existence. The *Junkers* were, in fact, in a quandary; they could only cultivate their estates with Slav labour, but by doing so they risked aggravating the population ratio between the Slav and Teutonic elements. Even so, recourse to immigrant labour

[5] *Germany's Eastern Neighbours:* E. Wiskemann (London, 1956), pp.11-14
[6] *Hitler Speaks:* H. Rauschning (London, 1939), p.140

was necessary; in 1912 the *Reichstag* noted with alarm that the Prussian economy virtually depended on a seasonal influx of some 750,000 workers, mostly from Russian Poland.[7] The migrant worker, or *Gastarbeiter*, is no new phenomenon.

The second factor that increasingly and adversely affected Russo-German relations was the growth of Pan-Slavism and the Pan-Germanism that was, in turn, provoked. Where German communities, some as far east as the Volga, had long flourished, new pressures began to be felt. Even in the Baltic provinces, in which ethnic Germans had made exceptional contributions to Russian administration and military prowess, discrimination was felt. Between 1881 and 1897 the German element in the Latvian province fell by forty per cent.[8] At the end of the nineteenth century there were still 1.8 million ethnic Germans (*Volksdeutschen*) in Russia outside the Baltic provinces, many of them forming closed communities, the prototypes of the armed peasantry (*Wehrbauern*) beloved of SS theorists; but their survival as islands of Germanic culture seemed less and less secure. The question confronting apostles of Pan-Germanism was: should a rescue operation be mounted to bring the *Volksdeutschen* home, or should the frontiers of the Reich be expanded to embrace them?

A leading critic of Bismarck's Russophile foreign policy was Paul de Lagarde, one of the forerunners accoladed by the Nazis, who believed that Germany should expand to her 'natural boundaries' at the expense of Russia.[9] Another was Paul Rohrbach; he was, like Alfred Rosenberg, a Baltic German born and educated in Russia, who made his career in the Reich. During the First World War Rohrbach, a strong supporter of *Mittel-Europa* policy, 'stood for separation of the West Russian peoples from their Great Russian masters',[10] and advocated an in-

---

[7] *Germany's Eastern Neighbours*, op. cit., p.12n.
[8] *Teuton and Slav*, op. cit., p.304
[9] *Mitteleuropa:* H. C. Meyer (The Hague, 1955), p.31
[10] Ibid., p.272

dependent Ukraine and a Caucasian federation under German influence. These ideas, strongly foreshadowing those later promoted by Rosenberg, influenced the policies of General Max Hoffmann and the German Administration of the Occupied East (*Ober Ost*) in the last phase of the war. These included plans for German settlement and colonization in the East, such as were later elaborated in exaggerated form in Himmler's General Plan for the East (*Generalplan Ost*).[11] A post-war German historian has written of Hitler: 'Gas-chambers and death-camps did not of course exist before his time, but the general lines of his policy can be traced far back in history.'[12]

In the quarter-century between the withdrawal of Bismarck's guiding hand and the outbreak of the First World War it is possible to trace two mutually contradictory attitudes towards Russia, which we shall also find reflected in Hitler's thinking. On the one hand there was the contempt for Slavs and their administrative and technological incapacity, to which we have already referred; from this derived the conclusion, which the victories on the eastern front in 1914-18 tended to support, that Russia would fall an easy victim to German arms. On the other hand there was the uneasy fear that this might not long continue to be the case; that Russia would eventually emerge into the modern world and that, when this at last occurred, her immense resources of manpower would make her indestructible. At the beginning of the century a German population of 65 millions saw on its eastern borders a Colossus of 170 millions, growing in numbers at three times the German rate. Germany lacked natural frontiers and, as the war-time blockade was soon to demonstrate, lacked also the raw materials to sustain a long war. As Professor A. Hillgruber has so cogently put it: 'Social-Darwinist ideas of the irresistible growth of Russia and her potential, together with the racial (*voelkisch*) concept of the irreconcilable antagonism between the Slav and the German (originally represented in

[11] *Der Generalplan Ost:* H. Heiber (*VfZg*, Munich, 1958)
[12] *Teuton and Slav*, op. cit., p.319

the mind of the German ruling class well before the turn of the century), as well as the purely statistical way in which the Great German General Staff calculated Russian armed might, all led in their implications to the fatal conviction that Germany was becoming trapped.'[13]

Until Schlieffen became Chief of Staff in 1891, German plans to meet the dreaded two-front war had presupposed a first strike against Russia, whilst standing fast on the western front. Because of Russia's slow rate of mobilization and rudimentary transport system, Schlieffen reversed the order: Germany should strike with lightning speed in the west and achieve a knock-out blow before the Russian 'steam-roller' could gain momentum. Signs of Russian weakness during the 1904 war with Japan seemed to vindicate the new plan. Some held, however, that Germany had missed the chance to strike a preventive blow against Russia at that time. The failure to do so haunted Chancellor Bethmann Hollweg and after 1909 he was obsessed by his fear of the grave menace Russia would become when she had developed her full military and economic potential.

War, when it came, found the German General Staff prepared only for a short, decisive struggle. As stalemate froze the western front and the blockade began to pinch, hopes became concentrated on the east, where Hindenburg and Ludendorff, with increased forces after their elevation to plenary power in 1916, were conducting a war of movement. The rich natural resources of the Ukraine exerted their fascination upon the hungry German people. These had been forbidden pastures whilst an equal alliance with Austria had precluded development in that direction but, with the Habsburg empire on its deathbed and also dying of starvation, old restraints could be abandoned. The Ukraine must become a German granary. The province had declared its independence as early as July 1917 and had its own delegation sitting at the Brest-Litovsk conference alongside the Bolsheviks. When nego-

---

[13] *Deutschlands Rolle in der Vorgeschichte der beiden Weltkriege:* A. Hillgruber (Goettingen, 1967), p.25

tiations with the latter were broken off, the Germans signed a separate peace treaty with the Ukraine Rada early in February 1918. But why stop there? General Hoffmann resumed the offensive against the Red Army with the slogan, 'For the protection of Finland, Estonia, Livonia and Ukraine!'[14] When peace was finally signed at Brest-Litovsk in March 1918, German forces had penetrated to the Crimea and Baku. In the following months Germany also recognized the independence of Georgia, and the Kaiser in a message to the Hetman of the Don Cossacks outlined plans for the 'ultimate partitioning of Russia into four independent states – the Ukraine, the Union of the South-East, Central Russia and Siberia . . .'[15] Puppet Grand Duchies were also to be set up in Courland, Estonia, Lithuania and Livonia. This area and the Ukraine, under German economic domination, would become an autarky, largely independent of the outside world. In this cauldron the broth of future Nazi eastern policy was cooked.

The triumph of Brest-Litovsk, by which Germany claimed the right to determine the fate of some 55 million inhabitants of former Tsarist provinces, was short-lived; Lenin denounced the Treaty two days after Germany had signed the armistice at Compiègne. The Entente also annulled the Treaty, but the last thing they wanted was to see Bolshevism spreading along the Baltic coast, and German troops were at first allowed to remain in the future Baltic Republics, which were seeking their independence. Some North Germans were prepared, if need be, to abandon the Rhineland to the French and defy the Treaty of Versailles, basing their defiance upon an Eastern State (*Oststaat*), which would include East and West Prussia and Silesia.[16] The determination of France to create a viable Poland was fatal to this desperate project. A Polish army of 90,000 men, equipped by France, was

[14] *The Forgotten Peace:* J. Wheeler-Bennett (New York, 1939), p.244
[15] Ibid., p.326
[16] *Der Oststaat-Plan:* H. Schulze (*VfZg*, Munich, 1970)

transported eastward and in the summer of 1919 resistance to the pattern imposed by Versailles came to an end – at least in an overt form.

Whilst German diplomatists in their acrimonious debates with the Entente were depicting Germany as the bulwark against Bolshevism, German generals were arguing that Germans and Russians should not shed one another's blood at the behest of France. General von Seeckt, who had distinguished himself on the eastern front, was opposed to fighting the Red Army. General Groener, who succeeded Ludendorff as Hindenburg's Quarter-Master General, agreed with him, adding, 'We must do what is required to secure Russia's friendship in the future.'[17] The infant German Republic refused in October 1919 to join the *Entente* in an economic blockade of the USSR; indeed Walther Rathenau and others were considering how best to promote economic co-operation between the two countries. At the end of the war both proved to be losers; both were excluded from the newly formed League of Nations, which Lenin dubbed 'League of Victors!'.

The incipient accord was clinched in April 1920 by Poland's invasion of the Ukraine. Seeckt prepared the first of several plans for invading Poland and, like other military men in Germany, was disappointed when the Poles, with French help, defeated the advancing Red Army before the gates of Warsaw. The rash advance of the Russians had disclosed many weaknesses; even before Russo-German diplomatic relations were resumed in May 1921 Lenin had proposed collaboration between the Red Army and the Reichswehr. Seeckt welcomed it; as he pithily said, 'Poland must disappear!'. Yet the Russo-German *rapprochement* rested upon the existence of Poland. The Treaty of Riga, concluded in 1921, had assigned to Poland some 6 million Ukrainians, some of them usually described as Galicians or Ruthenians, belonging not to the Orthodox but to the Uniate Church.

[17] *Unholy Alliance:* G. Freund (London, 1957), p.39

Once Germany had succeeded in breaking up Poland, these elements could be used as a lever to prise free the 30 million Ukrainians under Russian rule.

The threat lay dormant throughout the Weimar era, whilst semi-clandestine co-operation flourished between the German and Russian armed forces. This is a story that has been related often and well and need not be repeated here. The marriage between the Prussian *Junkers* and the Bolsheviks was one of convenience; the Reichswehr saw no inconsistency in suppressing communism at home, whilst exploiting in the USSR the opportunities for circumventing the restrictions on rearmament and training imposed by Versailles. Contacts with the Red Army, which were close and even cordial at times, did not make senior German officers sympathetic towards the Soviet system, though we have it on the authority of Rauschning that General von Blomberg, who visited the USSR when serving under Groener in the Weimar Ministry of Defence, was so impressed by the national discipline attainable in a one-party state that he became well-disposed to Hitler.[18]

Seeckt provided for the disoriented officer corps the necessary sense of continuity between the stable politics of the Second Reich and the democratic hurly-burly of the detestable Republic. When he said that the Reichswehr should be non-political, he meant only that it should take its politics from him. The programme was simple: Germany must again become strong; the Versailles settlement must be overthrown; and the means to these desirable ends lay in working closely with Russia. In this doctrine he brought up the generation of General Staff officers whom Hitler inherited in 1933. It was the creed of General Heye, who succeeded Seeckt in 1926; it was that of General von Hammerstein, who followed Heye in 1930 and in 1931 attended Soviet manoeuvres held with airborne troops. The same views were shared by his friend, General von Schleicher, who briefly preceded Hitler as Chancellor.

[18] *The German General Staff:* W. Goerlitz (London, 1953), p.233

Hitler agreed, of course, that Germany must again become strong and must throw off the shackles of Versailles; but he wholly rejected collaboration with Russia. In December 1932 he explained his attitude in a letter to Colonel von Reichenau, who later became one of his Field-Marshals and died of a heart-attack in the first winter of the invasion of Russia. Hitler wrote that he had opposed for many years closer relations with Russia and had so informed Hammerstein. It was a political connection that made 'the rest of the world unsympathetic' – a phrase that half-revealed his hope of an alliance with Britain. In any case, he added, 'Russia is not a state, but a *Weltanschauung*, which is for the present confined to that territory . . .'[19] But Hitler's ideological views and Nazi foreign policy require a chapter of their own.

[19] *Hitlers Brief an Reichenau:* T. Vogelsang (*VfZg*, Munich, 1959)

# II

## Ideology and Foreign Policy

At Nuremberg after the war Hitler's imprisoned paladins
were in no doubt where responsibility for the disaster
had lain. 'Foreign policy above all,' said Goering, 'was
the Fuehrer's very own realm.'[1] Rosenberg was more
emotive: 'Never did the Great-German dream seem
nearer to realization than in 1938. Yet never did the
Reich collapse in more total ruin than in 1945. All that is
summed up in *one* name . . .'[2] Even if the major war
criminals in 1945 were still hoping to evade their share
of responsibility, on this issue at least we can accept their
evidence. This is not, of course, the same as saying that
Hitler at all times had complete freedom of action. When
he first came to power, he was severely hampered in the
two fields in which he most wished to exert himself –
foreign and military policy. After the death of Hindenburg
and the success of Hitler's first initiatives, his autocracy
expanded rapidly, until by the late summer of 1938 the
chances of legitimately influencing him were reckoned to
be so slight by the group round Beck and Goerdler, who
chiefly wished to do so, that they went underground;
from that time active resistance had to be covert.

By 1940-1 Hitler stood at the summit of his power
and success, both inside and outside Germany. This did
not mean that he could take decisions in entire disregard
of the views of those who would have to execute them;
he had sensitive antennae and knew very well where
passive resistance lurked and needed to be overcome.
The Fuehrer cult had accustomed him to the idea – at
once gratifying and exasperating – that lesser mortals
might fail to respond with instant enthusiasm and un-
questioning loyalty to his breadth of vision and the vistas

[1] *International Military Tribunal*, Vol. IX, p.400
[2] *Grossdeutschland: Traum und Tragoedie*: ed. H. Haertle
(Munich, 1970), p.269

of unremitting struggle that it revealed. This was especially true of recalcitrant staff officers, reared in an obsolete, aristocratic tradition; their misgivings did not deflect him from his purposes, but did cause him, as time went on, to disclose his plans one stage at a time, using arguments calculated to appeal to his hearers, whether or not these represented his true motives.

Truth, indeed, had never been of the least interest to Hitler and after the winter of 1941, when his plans had gone gravely awry, he tended increasingly to try to preserve his infallibility by misleading those around him about his earlier intentions and the way in which these had supposedly been frustrated by the folly and disloyalty of others. His words carried the more conviction because he was an accomplished actor, as one might expect from the fact that among his entourage he passed as a good mimic. As he was also a master of deception, he succeeded in leaving a number of false trails, some of which have continued to confuse historians. For this reason we must begin this chapter with an account of the sources to be used in depicting Hitler's *Weltanschauung*, the evolution of his master-plan (to which Professor Andreas Hillgruber has given the name *Stufenplan*),[3] and the motives underlying the fatal decision to invade Russia.

What has been written above leaves us in the awkward situation of being unable to place implicit trust either in what Hitler himself wrote or said, or in what others have said and written about him. In this morass of mistrust, however, it is legitimate to regard some stepping-stones as more solid than others. Whilst treating all Hitler's public utterances with suspicion, especially those made after he came to power, we can be less sceptical about *Mein Kampf*, which he wrote at a time when his chances of ever becoming a responsible statesman were remote, and about the Second Book, which he never published.[4] Then there are the remarks he made in the intimate circle

---

[3] *Hitlers Strategie, Politik u. Kriegsfuehrung:* A. Hillgruber (Frankfurt, 1965)
[4] *Hitler's Secret Book:* ed. T. Taylor (New York, 1961)

of those whose minds he believed – sometimes erroneously – had been conditioned by exposure to his hypnotic power, or who had been corrupted by the bribes and favours he bestowed. With such men he liked to relax by letting fall the mask to some extent and talking more freely than at other times about his past triumphs and future plans.

The evidence of men who have been wholly corrupted is of doubtful value, but there are two witnesses in whom we can place credence. One is Hermann Rauschning, about whom Hitler made one of his rare mistakes; his account of Hitler's conversations covers the short, but vital, period 1932-4.[5] The other is Albert Speer, who was indeed corrupted, but in the long years in Spandau made a remarkable effort to cleanse his mind of prejudice and self-justification; his account is particularly useful for the years 1942-5.[6] In addition there are the verbatim records of Hitler's table talk,[7] which come into our preferred category of evidence, and also, though to a lesser degree, the reports of his briefing meetings with his generals, especially Keitel and Jodl, whose minds had certainly been conditioned beyond repair.[8]

These sources are not, of course, entirely dependable on all counts. For example, neither in *Mein Kampf*, nor in later conversations did Hitler give an honest account of his early life in Vienna. Moreover, like other self-appointed prophets and Messianic figures, he was markedly disinclined to give credit for his inspired ideas and utterances to others, especially if the latter were still living. The tributes in *Mein Kampf* to Karl Lueger and Dietrich Eckart are attributable, at least in part, to the fact that both were dead. Finally, Hitler's talk about those who served him was usually malicious and vindictive,

[5] *Hitler Speaks:* H. Rauschning (London, 1939)
[6] *Inside the Third Reich:* A. Speer (London, 1970)
[7] *Hitler's Table Talk:* ed. H. Trevor-Roper (London, 1953; *Hitlers Tischgespraeche:* ed. A. Hillgruber (Munich, 1968)
[8] *Lagebesprechungen im Fuehrerhauptquartier:* ed. H. Heiber (Stuttgart, 1962)

even beyond their deserts. This tendency was encouraged by his entourage, partly as relief from the tedium of constant repetition, and partly as a means of denigrating potential rivals.

When all this dross has been discarded, there does emerge a consistent line of thought or, as it would perhaps be better to put it, certain preconceptions about the life of man on earth and, in particular, about the history and destiny of Germanic and so-called Aryan peoples. These prejudices, dogmatically conceived and adhered to, were at all times present in Hitler's consciousness, even if often half-submerged, and must therefore be regarded as having influenced all his major decisions, some of which cannot be explained except in these terms. They were linked together in a way that justified Hitler's references to them as constituting a *Weltanschauung*. We shall describe them in these pages, for convenience, as an ideology, without further defining the various senses in which this word has been used. We cannot here follow all the tangled skeins of Hitler's ideological thinking, but shall single out those having a relationship to the culminating decision of his career, the decision to invade Russia that, indeed, put an end to his career.

Hitler's views of man's fate on earth have usually been summed up by the term Social-Darwinism. Life, he believed, consisted of perpetual struggle, in the course of which individuals and tribal and racial groups that grew weak, especially if they showed infirmity of will, were doomed to perish at the hands of the stronger. If, he wrote in his Second Book, 'politics is history in the making and history itself the presentation of the struggle of men and nations for self-preservation and continuance, then politics is in truth the execution of a nation's struggle for existence'.[9] It followed that war was not only an inevitable feature of human existence, but also a necessary one, since it served to maintain the required tension in national life. As he wrote in *Mein Kampf*, 'Man has be-

---

[9] *Secret Book*, op. cit., p.7

come great through perpetual struggle. In perpetual peace his greatness must decline.'[10]

A life of peace and relaxation of effort was not the only cause of decline; equally important was impurity of race, leading to that form of total degeneration which the renegade Englishman, Houston Stewart Chamberlain, had called 'racial chaos' (*Voelkerchaos*). Hitler believed that it was his historic mission to save from this fate not only the German people, but also any other Aryan people, whose racial purity was not already damaged beyond reprieve. Since race, as he used the word, was not a scientific concept, there was no objective way of determining at what point putative Aryans, such as the English, became incapable of salvation. Like his mentor, H. S. Chamberlain, Hitler's criteria were entirely subjective; the chief test was the reaction of the other nations to Hitler's policies. Thus England, which in *Mein Kampf* and the Second Book had been depicted as a suitable ally, had by about 1938 fallen victim to 'finance capital' and the Jews; the conclusive proof of this was shown by Britain's willingness after 1941 to fight as an ally of Soviet Russia against Germany.

Hitler's racial prejudices were those of a lower middle-class member of the German minority in Austria, which felt itself increasingly threatened by other ethnic groups. Traditional Germanic dominance was menaced, as he wrote in *Mein Kampf*, 'by a motley of Czechs, Poles, Hungarians, Serbs and Croats, etc., and always that bacillus which is the solvent of human society, the Jew . . .'[11] There was a strong Manichaean element in Hitler's doctrine; whilst the Aryans represented the forces of light, the Jews at the opposite pole were the forces of darkness (*Gegenrasse*). Before describing the syllogism, by which the Jews were identified with Bolsheviks, we must first add to this brief recital of Hitler's basic

[10] *Mein Kampf*: A. Hitler (trans. J. Murphy: London, 1939), p.124
[11] Ibid., p.114

beliefs the concept of *Lebensraum*, by which race was linked to soil (*Blut und Boden*).

Since to safeguard and promote the growth and prosperity of the Germanic peoples was the first duty of the responsible leader, it followed that their birth rate must not be in any way restricted; the frontiers and resources of the state must therefore expand to accommodate the growing population. The NSDAP programme issued in 1920, before the ideology was fully formulated, was ambiguous on the direction of expansion, implying indeed that at least part of the surplus population might be settled in the colonies: 'We demand land and territory (colonies) for the nourishment of our people and for settling our surplus population.'[12] This ambiguity had disappeared by the time Hitler came to write *Mein Kampf*; he rejected the idea of allowing Germany to be weakened by emigration overseas for two main reasons. One was that 'a commercial and colonial policy' would again bring Germany into conflict with Britain; but the second, more important, reason was connected with what the Nazis called 'race hygiene', as well as with their historic mission in Eastern Europe. 'Too much importance cannot be placed,' he wrote, 'on the necessity for adopting a policy which will make it possible to maintain a healthy peasant class as the basis of the national community.'[13] The profits of trade and industry would not only fail to compensate for the diminution of the peasantry, but would be positively harmful; the land would be neglected and the former cultivators would drift into the cities and fall victims to the *Voelkerchaos* that prevailed there.

There was, however, another, deeper motive for expansion eastward across the continental land mass; its mainspring was the mystical union between the race and the soil once cultivated by its forefathers, the soil where their blood had been shed. As Hitler wrote in *Mein Kampf*, 'What has been beneficially Germanized in the course of history was the land which our ancestors conquered with

[12] *Hitler's Speeches:* ed. N. Baynes (Oxford, 1942), Vol. I, p.400
[13] *Mein Kampf*, op. cit., p.126

the sword and colonized with German tillers of the soil.'[14]
This was the magnetic pull, to which the Aryans, their
racial purity restored, would respond. From this point of
view the foreign policy of the Second Reich had been a
mistaken one. 'If new territory were to be acquired in
Europe it must have been mainly at Russia's cost, and
once again the new German Empire should have set out
on its march along the same road as was formerly trodden
by the Teutonic Knights, this time to acquire soil for the
German plough by means of the German sword . . .'[15]

Late in the 1914-18 war this realization had dawned
upon the German General Staff. Hitler had strongly approved of the Treaty of Brest-Litovsk; whilst still in the
army he had written a leaflet about it and the Treaty had
been the theme of many of his speeches when he first
joined the NSDAP. But the march to the east had come
too late to save Germany from the blockade, which was
itself due to the fatal error of incurring British hostility.
In the second volume of *Mein Kampf* the great objective
of Nazi foreign policy was clearly enunciated: 'We put
an end to the perpetual Germanic march towards the
South and West of Europe and turn our eyes towards the
land of the East . . . we must principally think of Russia
and the border States subject to her.'[16]

This policy may be criticized as immoral, but it does
not lack a certain logical coherence. The irrational element, introduced into it with such disastrous results in
the long run, was to equate the Bolshevik leaders of
Russia with the Jews, the anti-race. This was not a part
of the collective beliefs of all the early Nazis; indeed the
young party had had connections with the so-called
National Bolsheviks, who advocated a radical programme
of social and economic reform, whilst rejecting the inter-
nationalist aspect of Marxism. This Party faction was
pro-Russian and, because anti-imperialist, anti-British. It
was never strong in Bavaria, but attracted most of its

[14] Ibid., p.328
[15] Ibid., p.128
[16] Ibid., p.533

adherents in the 'Red' Ruhr, where during the interregnum of Hitler's imprisonment the Strasser brothers and Goebbels were able to operate in virtual independence of Munich. As late as February 1926 Goebbels wrote in his diary, referring to Hitler's opening speech at the Bamberg conference: 'Russian question: altogether beside the point. Italy and Britain the natural allies. Horrible!'[17] Goebbels was soon after won over, but the Party was not finally purged of its radical wing until 1930, when Otto Strasser was expelled. The NSDAP in its propaganda continued to the end of its days to attack 'international finance capital'; but this was no longer economic policy, but racial policy. The capitalism of world Jewry completed the 'Communist – Jew: Plutocrat – Jew' syllogism.

In attempting to explain the first half of the syllogism, it must be stressed at the outset that it did not seem as irrational immediately after the First World War as it does today. Trotsky, Zinoviev and (at least in Germany) Radek – all Jewish – were notorious figures in the Russian revolution. In Hungary 'Red' revolution was connected with Bela Kun and Szamuely. The Independent Socialist regime in Bavaria immediately after the War was led by a Jew, Kurt Eisner, who paid the price with his life, as Rathenau was to do later. There was a high proportion of Jews, including Russians, in the short-lived Munich Soviet in the spring of 1919. Moreover, Jews and Marxists were linked together by those in Germany who propagated the legend of the 'stab in the back' to exculpate the army from the ignominy of having lost the war. These 'November Criminals', as Nazi propaganda loved to call them, were widely held by the whole of the Right to be guilty of having lost the war on the home front.

The mythical identification, however, between Jews and Bolsheviks did not originate in Germany, but in Tsarist Russia, where it served the sinister purposes of the Okhrana, or secret police, and of elements in the Orthodox Church. It was part of the stock in trade of

[17] *The Early Goebbels Diaries:* ed. H. Heiber (London, 1962): entry of 15.2.1926

the 'Black Hundreds', anti-semitic and patriotic groups, who organized pogroms and terrorized those who showed signs of political dissidence.[18] The 'Black Hundreds', which disintegrated after the October Revolution in Russia, were the true prototype of the SS; their evil legacy was carried to Germany after the war in the baggage of 'White Russian' refugees from Bolshevism. The most influential carrier of this bacillus to be associated with Hitler and the NSDAP was Alfred Rosenberg, who was born in 1893, probably of German stock, in Reval (later Tallinn) then capital of the Estonian province of Russia. Baltic German landowners and traders had been an object of revolutionary hostility in the abortive risings of 1905, in which a number of Jews had been prominent. Rosenberg, who completed his studies as an architect in Moscow in 1918, became both anti-semitic and anti-communist and made a speech in the Reval Town Hall, linking these twin threats to civilization, before going to Germany with the retreating German troops at the end of November 1918.[19] In Munich he attached himself to Dietrich Eckart, who was already active in anti-semitic and anti-communist propaganda, and between them they exerted an influence on the still impressionable mind of Hitler, who had just been discharged from the army and was embarking on a political career. When Eckart died in December 1923, he left unfinished a booklet purporting to summarize conversations between Hitler and himself; it was published in the following year under the title *Bolshevism from Moses to Lenin: Dialogue between Hitler and Myself* by a subsidiary of the NSDAP publishing house, the Eher *Verlag*. Hitler, when he came to power, called in as many copies as could be traced, but he never disowned the book or its author.[20]

Why was Hitler so ready to accept the Jew-Bolshevik syndrome against the inclinations of an important section of the Party? One reason was that it fitted so conveniently

[18] *Warrant for Genocide:* N. Cohn (London, 1967), pp.120-2
[19] *Myth of the Master Race:* R. Cecil (London, 1972), p.20
[20] *Bolschevismus von Moses bis Lenin:* D. Eckart (Munich, 1924)

with his determination to secure *Lebensraum* in the East; those who wished to march against the Slavs and seize their lands could make common cause with those wishing to exterminate the Jews. Secondly, it corresponded to one of the basic principles of his propaganda that the message should be made as simple as possible and that the hatred whipped up among what he liked to call 'the broad masses' should, if possible, be directed against a single target. This analysis is not intended to suggest that Hitler presented this target simply in pursuance of cold calculation; on the contrary, it is clear that he was himself the first victim of his own propaganda, which echoed his deep anti-semitic, anti-Slav and anti-Marxist prejudices. Had this not been the case, he would, as war lord, have acted in a manner more consistent with the efficient achievement of rational political and strategic aims. He would not, for example, have diverted scarce resources and manpower to the extermination of the Jews until the war had been won. He would have fought the war in the East in much the same way as he had fought in the West; that is, he would have exploited opportunities for political warfare and would not have pursued genocidal policies against the Slavs, which virtually precluded termination of hostilities on any terms other than total victory or total defeat.

Above all, as we shall hope in the following pages to show, he would not have attacked Russia in so contemptuous a manner and with such exaggerated expectations of quick triumph. For implicit in the Jew-Bolshevik identification was the assumption that the defects ascribed by Hitler to Jews also afflicted the Bolsheviks. Chief among these defects was the inability to create and maintain a state; the Jew-Bolshevik could destroy, but not construct. In Hitler's view, such progress as had been achieved in Tsarist Russia had in any case been due to the influence of imported Aryan groups; these the Revolution had decimated. 'It was not as if the Slav race instinct had deliberately carried out the struggle for the extermination of the former non-Russian upper stratum by itself. No, it had acquired new leaders meantime in Jewry.'[21] By definition the new leadership would not be able to bring order out of chaos. It was for this reason that, 'This colossal Empire in the East is ripe for dissolution. And the end of the Jewish domination in Russia will also be the end of Russia as a state. We are chosen by Destiny to be the witnesses of a catastrophe which will afford the strongest confirmation of the nationalist theory of race.'[22]

It should not, of course, be supposed that all Nazis shared such views, especially in the extreme form in which Hitler expressed them, both in private and in his published work. There was, however, one powerful group which wholeheartedly espoused them and dedicated itself not merely to witnessing the coming catastrophe in the East, but to precipitating it. Heinrich Himmler had belonged as a young man to the Artamanen League, which aimed to resettle the depopulated eastern provinces with German peasantry. Quite apart from his personal devotion to Hitler, Himmler was predisposed to accept this line of ideological thinking. His enthusiasm was reinforced by that of Walther Darre, another of the Nazi leaders born outside the Reich, who before joining the SS had been a civil servant in the Prussian Ministry of Agriculture and in 1931 published a book on *The Peasantry as Prime Source of the Nordic Race*.[23] In the same year Himmler made him head of the SS Race and Settlement Main Office, which was responsible for elaborating the plans that were later applied so ruthlessly in Poland. Darre, who had become Reich Minister of Agriculture in 1933, fell out with Himmler and quit his SS post in 1938; Himmler described him as too theoretical, meaning that Darre could not entirely overcome his repugnance for genocide in its practical application.

Those who helped Himmler after he became, on the

[21] *Secret Book*, op. cit., p.138
[22] *Mein Kampf*, op. cit., p.533
[23] *Das Bauerntum als Urquell der nordischen Rasse:* W. Darre (Munich, 1929)

outbreak of war, Reich Commissar for Reinforcing Germandom (RKFDV), were less squeamish. After the invasion of Russia it was their task to fan out into territory where there had long been ethnic German minorities and to reinforce these by injecting good Germanic blood from areas such as the Italian Tyrol, from which it had become convenient to promote emigration.[24] The SS, in pursuing this policy, was consciously harking back to a more primitive period of history, as we can read in one of the leaflets that they issued: 'But what the Goths, the Varangians and all the individual wanderers of Germanic blood could not do, that we shall achieve: our Fuehrer, the Fuehrer of all Germans, will now accomplish it – a new march of the Germans. Now the assault from the steppes will be thrown back; now the eastern frontier of Europe will finally be assured; now the ancient dream of the Germanic fighters in the woods and wastes of the East will come true. A chapter of history that has lasted 3,000 years reaches today its glorious conclusion. Since 22 June 1941 the Goths ride again – every one of us a Germanic fighter!'[25]

[24] *RKFDV: German Resettlement Policy:* R. L. Koehl (Harvard, 1957), pp.148ff.
[25] *Der Nationalsozialismus: Dokumente:* ed. W. Hofer (Frankfurt, 1957), p.250

# III

## Hitler and His Army

Before we begin to analyse the strategic situation facing Hitler in the critical summer of 1940, we must first consider his relationship to his army and, in particular, to the officer corps. For this relationship is highly relevant to three questions: what Hitler felt he could demand of the military machine; what account of his intentions he was prepared to disclose to his generals; and to what extent they were able to influence his decisions. It was a relationship that had undergone successive transformations since Hitler was released from the army as a lance-corporal (*Gefreiter*) at the end of March 1920. At that date the war had been the great emotional experience of Hitler's life and there is no reason to doubt his expressions of solidarity with his fellow soldiers and admiration for the German army as a whole. In *Mein Kampf* he describes it as 'the great school of the German nation'[1] and praises its organization and leadership as 'the most mighty thing that the world has ever seen'.[2]

There is no evidence suggesting that at this stage of his career he harboured a grudge, or feeling of inferiority, towards the officer corps, though admittedly it would have been in his nature to do so. In his secret book he criticizes Seeckt for having failed to prevent 'the removal of hardened, deliberately national-minded officers'[3] – presumably an allusion to the dissolution on the orders of the Republic of the various Free Corps. He also makes clear his opposition to any kind of alliance with Russia, though without specifically mentioning the close connection between the Reichswehr and Red Army, which Seeckt had so vigorously promoted. Before writing his books, Hitler had lived through the abortive Munich

[1] *Mein Kampf*, op. cit., p.236
[2] Ibid., p.196
[3] *Secret Book*, op. cit., pp.84-5

*Putsch*, which had failed largely because of the refusal of the military leadership in Bavaria, after some hesitation, to give its support. Whilst this episode cannot have endeared the officer caste to him, it did serve to convince him that he must cultivate its sympathy, since without its acquiescence he would never come to power.

This conclusion was underscored by the election in 1925 of President Hindenburg, who intended to be Commander-in-Chief in fact, as well as in name, and who, unlike his predecessor, was cordially welcomed in both his civil and military capacities by the army. The attitude of Hindenburg towards Hitler was much as might have been expected from the contrast between their social status and their military careers. The President usually referred to the younger man as the 'Bohemian lance-corporal', under the mistaken impression that Hitler had been born at Braunau in Bohemia. Hindenburg resented having to run twice against Hitler in the presidential elections of the spring of 1932, in the course of which Nazi propaganda made much of the contrast between the two men by presenting Hitler as the brave, simple front-line soldier, standing for the common man against aristocracy and entrenched privilege. Hindenburg's brusque treatment of Hitler later that year in his struggle for the Chancellorship certainly hurt his pride. He also resented the attempt of Schleicher to split the NSDAP by negotiating with Gregor Strasser. At the eleventh hour before Hitler at last became Chancellor his most acute apprehension was that he might be forestalled by a military coup, organized by Schleicher and his friend Hammerstein, who was Army Commander (*Chef der Heeresleitung*) and no friend of the Nazis. By this date the ground-work had been laid for a future relationship chiefly characterized by mutual suspicion.

Hitler's first private meeting after he came to power with his top-ranking naval and military commanders took place at the beginning of February 1933 at Hammerstein's house. Hitler spoke of his aims with considerable candour, even revealing in bald outline the first two stages of his

master plan. First the struggle against Versailles, for
which allies would be necessary, then 'conquest in the
East of new living-space, which was to be ruthlessly
Germanized'.[4] But significantly he justified this course of
action mainly on economic grounds, rather than by stressing the ideological argument, with which his hearers
could not have been expected to have much sympathy. If
his remarks failed to arouse their apprehensions, it was
because it seemed to them that the crusade in the East
lay in the distant future. Whilst they welcomed Hitler's
intention to give greater emphasis to rearmament, they
expected to be able to impose on it their own more
cautious timetable. Moreover they were well aware that it
was precisely in the areas of foreign and military policy
that Hindenburg, by appointing Neurath and Blomberg
to the key posts, had erected a barrier against Hitler's
rash ambitions. How ineffective it would prove to be was
well summed up in the soubriquet soon earned by Blomberg – 'the rubber lion'.

The point of more immediacy in Hitler's oration, on
which his hearers must have fastened, was his assurance
that he did not intend to fuse the army with the much
larger body of Storm Troopers (SA). This decision,
which Hitler reaffirmed a year later in more specific
terms, was crucial not only to the development of the
army, but also to the evolution of the Third Reich. It
ended Roehm's hopes of a People's Army, permeated
with the Nazi community spirit, in place of the Reichswehr which, because of the way in which its officer corps
was recruited, must remain a bastion of the traditional
elite. Before the end of 1933 Roehm had become highly
critical of Hitler: 'Adolf is a swine . . . getting matey
with the East Prussian Generals . . . you won't make a
revolutionary army out of the old Prussian NCOs . . .
afterwards he'll make National-Socialists of them, he
says!'[5] By 1944 Hitler had still not achieved this objective. Roehm paid with his life for his opposition and, im-

[4] *Der Nationalsozialismus*, op. cit., pp.180-1
[5] *Hitler Speaks*, op. cit., pp.154-5

mediately after the 'Night of the Long Knives', it must have seemed to the Generals that the elimination of their leading rival and the assurance that they alone would wield the power of the sword had fortified their position, even though the murder of Schleicher and the removal of Hammerstein perturbed some of them. The fragility of this optimism was exposed some five weeks later, when the death of Hindenburg lifted the cover under which they had been sheltering and Hitler seized the chance to bind them to him as *Fuehrer* with a new oath of loyalty, cast in the most unconditional terms. By August 1934 with Goering already building up the Luftwaffe in the spirit of Nazism and Himmler planning to develop the military arm of the SS (*Waffen-SS*), Hitler's earlier assurances to the Generals had begun to sound very hollow. The introduction of conscription in March 1935, whilst welcome to the Generals as a means of expanding the armed forces, tended in the long run to weaken their hold on the military machine, as Hitler's successes at home and abroad fed his popularity among the German people.

Apart from the tempo of rearmament, the main point at issue in these early days between Hitler and the military leadership concerned eastern policy. As has already been pointed out, the 'special relationship' between Reichswehr and Red Army, which had been integrated into the foreign policy of the Weimar Republic, had rested upon the hostility of both parties to Poland. This pattern had become ingrained in the German military mind. Blomberg, who had become Hitler's Minister of Defence, referred after the war to the elimination of Poland as 'a sacred duty'.[6] General v. Fritsch, who at the end of 1933 replaced Hammerstein, was also a hater of Poland and a keen supporter of the connection with the Red Army. Fritsch appointed as his Chief of Staff another soldier in the old tradition, Ludwig Beck.

Hitler loved neither Russians nor Poles, but so long as Germany was weak he could hardly afford to offend both. His accession to power had aroused alarm in the Kremlin,

[6] *IMT*, Vol. XXXII, 3704-PS

where Rosenberg's influence was overestimated and his contact with Ukrainian emigrés was watched with anxiety. Hitler was not prepared to curb the anti-communist propaganda of the NSDAP, but he did renew the 1926 Berlin Treaty of Mutual Non-Aggression with the USSR. The threat from Poland was more immediate; Marshal Pilsudski, whose army was more than twice the size of the Reichswehr, was believed to have proposed to the French a preventive war against the Third Reich. Hitler was prepared to bide his time; in any case Austria and Czechoslovakia came before Poland in his table of priorities for the revision of Versailles. Demand for Danzig was muted and Pilsudski, after failing to obtain a positive response in Paris, agreed to a Non-Aggression Pact with Germany, which was signed in January 1934. Meanwhile the extensive installations of the Reichswehr in the USSR had been liquidated and in the autumn of 1933 the last of the annual banquets was held, marking the October Revolution, and the last toast to the Red Army was drunk by the senior Reichswehr officers who were present.[7] Stalin and Litvinoff lost no time in bringing about a *rapprochement* with France, and the USSR joined the League of Nations, from which Germany had withdrawn.

The older generation of army officers was made uneasy by these developments. In the aftermath of the 'Night of the Long Knives' and the murder of Schleicher, Hammerstein joined with the old Field-Marshal v. Mackensen in submitting to Hindenburg a memorandum of protest, in which they recommended, among other things, that Hitler should abandon his 'pro-Polish policy' and return to that of Rapallo; thirty Generals and senior General Staff officers appended their signatures.[8] But Hindenburg was past influencing events and the only effect on Hitler was to increase his contempt for the political acumen of the General Staff, who had failed to follow his tactics. As Germany became stronger, the anti-

[7] *German General Staff*, op. cit., p.279
[8] *The Nemesis of Power:* J. Wheeler-Bennett (London, 1953), p.329

communist propaganda of the NSDAP grew indistinguishable from anti-Russian propaganda. At the end of November 1936 Ribbentrop signed with the Japanese Ambassador in Berlin the Anti-Comintern Pact, which threatened a pincer-movement against the USSR, even though that country was not specified by name; the Pact was transformed in the following year into an international Fascist bloc – at least on paper – by the adherence of Italy.

These developments were not to the liking of the Generals. When the Spanish Civil War broke out in 1936, Blomberg and Fritsch opposed intervention at the side of Italy; they did not believe Germany was ready to reach out for hegemony in Europe, let alone a role in world power politics. Hitler and Goering overruled them, just as they overruled Schacht and the other economic experts, who tried to insist that the pace of rearmament be slowed down. (See Chapter IX.) Early in November 1937 Hitler decided that the time had come to disclose to Neurath, Blomberg and his three Service Commanders-in-Chief another phase of his master-plan with the intention of either carrying them with him, or replacing them by more devoted, or pliable, men. The record of the dialogue that resulted is the one that takes its familiar name from Hitler's military adjutant, Colonel Hossbach. Much of what Hitler had to say on this occasion was already known to his hearers – the economic and population pressures on the Third Reich and the need to solve these by seizing the required living space in his own life-time; but a new note of urgency intruded. If Britain and France were pre-occupied or indifferent, a lightning move against Czechoslovakia might even be made in the coming year.[9] Moreover a new note of self-confidence entered into Hitler's remarks about Britain and her Empire; his fading hopes of an alliance had led not to a modification of his plans, but to a determination to pursue these, if not with Britain, then in despite of her. The curtain was briefly lifted on the vista of world conquest.

[9] *Documents on German Foreign Policy*, Series D, Vol. I, p.29

The impact on the hearers, other than Goering, who had heard it all before, was not to inspire, but to alarm. Even if little was said, it was enough for Hitler. Almost exactly three months later Neurath, Blomberg and Fritsch were removed, together with a recalcitrant diplomatist, Ulrich v. Hassell, the Ambassador in Rome, and no fewer than sixteen Generals of the Seeckt tradition. Hossbach was also replaced for showing sympathy with Fritsch. Neurath was ceremoniously kicked upstairs; Blomberg's unsuitable marriage was at least a pretext for his dismissal; but the fabrication by the Security Service (*Sicherheitsdienst* – SD) of evidence of homosexuality against Fritsch was a calculated insult to the corps of senior officers. Though Fritsch was later vindicated, he was not given a command and met his end, apparently at his own wish, in the Polish campaign.

Before examining the failure of the army to make any collective protest, we must first consider the effect of Blomberg's retirement upon the command structure, which thereafter remained virtually unchanged until Fritsch's successor, General (later Field-Marshal) v. Brauchitsch, was removed in December 1941 and Hitler took direct command of the army. A number of developments had combined to make the problem of the military hierarchy an intractable one. In the first place, the character of warfare had so changed that the concept of separate civilian and military control of two self-contained sectors of national life in time of war had become obsolete. In 1916 the Hindenburg-Ludendorff duumvirate had taken supreme control under the Kaiser's nominal suzerainty. Below the duumvirate the General Staff was responsible for the uniform strategic direction of the war. The abdication of the Kaiser decapitated the military body; a popularly elected civilian President could hardly have replaced him in time of war, even if the Reichswehr had been willing to tolerate such a situation. The military body had been further emasculated by the ostensible abolition of the General Staff, in accordance with the Treaty of Versailles.

When Hitler came to power, with a former Field-Marshal as President and a serving soldier as Minister of Defence, something approximating to the traditional structure had been restored in practice; but two problems at once arose, quite apart from Hindenburg's death in 1934. One was Goering's determination, in defiance of Versailles, to create an Air Force and administer it in complete independence of the covertly reconstituted General Staff; the Navy inevitably followed his example. The second factor was the duality between the staff of the soldier-Minister and that of the army commander (*Oberbefehlshaber des Heeres*) and his Chief of Staff, who aspired to retain the general direction of rearmament and strategic planning, not only for the army, but for the other Services as well. The shortages of foreign currency and imported raw materials, which soon developed, and the pressures on available man-power, which intensified later, aggravated the rivalries and administrative confusion. Indeed one cause of the meeting recorded by Hossbach was certainly Hitler's vain hope that, by injecting an increased sense of urgency, he could induce Blomberg, Goering and Raeder to pull together, instead of pulling against one another.[10] A reorganization at the top was, therefore, overdue, quite apart from Hitler's dissatisfaction with the subordinate leadership in the fields of military and foreign policy.

The most prominent candidate – in every sense – for the succession to Blomberg was Goering. Nobody else backed him and Blomberg's suggestion that Hitler himself should take over his former functions was probably designed to forestall Goering's appointment. The name of Reichenau, who had at one time been high in Hitler's favour, was also considered, but turned down by the Fuehrer. It is not clear whether this was because Reichenau was already showing those signs of independence that later marked his behaviour, or whether Hitler thought that the appointment would too much offend the older Generals – not to mention Goering. (In 1933 Reichenau's

[10] *Arms, Autarky and Aggression:* W. Carr (London, 1972), p.73

candidature to succeed Hammerstein had had to be withdrawn, because Generals v. Rundstedt and v. Leeb had refused to serve under him.)[11] Reichenau was in many respects a strong contender; when Blomberg became Minister in 1933, Reichenau had taken charge under him of the politico-military functions of the Minister's Office (*Ministeramt*), which had been created to suit the special talents of Schleicher. Renamed the Armed Forces Office (*Wehrmachtamt*), it took over as its military staff the Department of National Defence (*Landesverteidigungsabteilung*) then headed by Hitler's fervent admirer Alfred Jodl. Both Reichenau and Jodl devoutly believed that there should be a body equivalent to the Combined Chiefs of Staff to undertake the central direction of a future war. When Hitler solved his problem by taking over as Supreme Commander of the Armed Forces, with Wilhelm Keitel as his Chief of Staff, Jodl was reassured and wrote in his diary: 'The unity of the armed forces is saved.'[12]

General Ludwig Beck, the Army Commander's Chief of Staff, agreed that unity of direction must be achieved, but would have brought it about by giving supremacy among the three Service Ministries to that representing the army, thus preserving the traditional authority of the army General Staff. The army commander would have had supreme command on land in time of war.[13] It should have been evident to him that this project had no chance of success; not only was it certain to incur the hostility of Goering and Raeder, but it would also have relegated Hitler to a status comparable to that of the Kaiser in the First World War. There was never the remotest chance that he would have accepted this; to have had the status without the power would have run contrary to 'the Fuehrer principle'. Moreover even before 1938 – his *annus mirabilis* – he had had no difficulty in convincing himself that, as a strategist, he was a match for any

[11] *German General Staff*, op. cit., p.282
[12] *Im Hauptquartier der deutschen Wehrmacht:* W. Warlimont (Frankfurt, 1964), p.25
[13] *German General Staff*, op. cit., p.298

*Junker*. As he had said earlier to Rauschning, 'I shall not allow myself to be ordered about by "Commanders-in-Chief". *I* shall make war . . .'[14]

It would probably be premature to pick on February 1938 as the date at which Hitler became disillusioned with his senior army officers; but he certainly had a mounting sense of grievance. Towards the end of 1939, after the highly successful Polish campaign, he listed his complaints in a frank conversation with General Guderian, who had replaced Reichenau in his favour. 'He started with the trouble Fritsch and Beck had caused him when he began the rearmament of Germany. He had wanted the immediate formation of 36 Divisions, but they had told him he must be satisfied for the time-being with 21. The Generals had warned him against the reoccupation of the Rhineland . . . Blomberg had proved a great disappointment to him, and the Fritsch incident had left a bitter taste in his mouth. Beck had opposed him during the Czech crisis and had therefore gone. The present Commander-in-Chief of the army had made proposals on the subject of further rearmament that were totally insufficient . . .'[15]

Although the main elements of this indictment must have been building up in Hitler's mind in February 1938, the solution that he then imposed was in the nature of a compromise and left a good deal of power in the hands of Beck and his successor, Franz Halder, of the Army High Command (OKH). Their control at working level over the army machine was unimpaired, even if they had had to abandon their hope of capturing the Department of National Defence from the new High Command of the Armed Forces (OKW) under Keitel. By selecting a nonentity, like Keitel, and making him equal, but not superior, to the Commanders of the three Services, Hitler had not, in fact, secured the unity of the armed forces. The threads came together in his hands, but at the level immediately below he had merely created a fourth channel

[14] *Hitler Speaks*, op. cit., p.20
[15] *Panzer Leader*: H. Guderian (London, 1952), p.87

through which limited authority could flow. The OKW had come into existence as a rival to the OKH; nothing resembling a Combined Chiefs of Staff had been set up.

In 1938, when the Cabinet had already ceased to meet, Hitler set up a Defence Cabinet, of which he was nominal chairman with Goering as his deputy. This body included the chief civil and military leaders and on the eve of war acquired a steering committee, or Council of Ministers for Defence, with Goering as chairman and Keitel the military member; but this body, which, on paper, could have played a useful role in co-ordinating civil and military requirements, never functioned effectively. In any case, it could not have assumed strategic direction of the war, because its military member, Keitel, was not recognized, even by Hitler, as having responsibility for representing and co-ordinating the three armed Services. The fact that Hitler was to take over in 1941 the personal direction of the army would further expose the deficiencies of the chain of command, since he alone could impose unified control, even in matters of less than the highest importance. That Hitler should become a politico-military war lord was imposed by the nature of the man and his situation; but that he should have been condemned to function with such a loosely co-ordinated machine was his own deliberate decision. It was to have formidable consequences.

Why did Hitler act in this way? The most plausible answer is that he was operating on the principle of 'divide and rule'; he certainly discouraged his military advisers from coming together for discussion among themselves; they were officially allowed to assemble only for the purpose of collectively hearing their master's voice. There may also have been in the untidy reorganization an element of his Austrian '*schlamperei*' – his distaste for neat administrative solutions. More importantly, however, he must have wished to avoid alienating the older Generals too far by imposing too drastic remedies. Although certainly capable of instant and ruthless decision, Hitler usually preferred to evade obstacles, as long as he could, rather than meet them head on. In 1938 he was helpless to carry out his plans without the co-operation of his Generals. Admittedly he could have sacked them all, instead of removing only sixteen (some of whom had to be re-employed when war broke out); but this would have meant accepting a slower tempo for fulfilment of his ambitions, whilst the younger generation of officers, more imbued with the Nazi spirit, was winning its spurs. When in March 1938 Hitler abruptly decided to move into Austria, the military machine was unprepared for so sudden a jab on the accelerator. It was, as Guderian put it, 'all a matter of improvisation . . .'[16] A strike of Generals, even unaccompanied by threats of open revolt, would have put an end to Hitler's adventurous policies – at least for the time-being.

It was in August 1938 that, under the influence of Beck, such a strike nearly came about. In the spring Beck had shown strong disapproval of Hitler's insistence on transforming into an offensive plan against Czechoslovakia the contingency plan that already existed to defend the Reich against a combined move by her potential enemies. He further underlined the disruptive nature of Hitler's military reform by calling a meeting of senior army officers to which no representative of OKW was invited.[17] When on 30 May 1938 the Fuehrer informed the military leadership of his 'unalterable decision that Czechoslovakia must be destroyed',[18] opposition grew, since many senior officers shared Beck's view that hostilities could not be restricted to Czechoslovakia and that the Reich was inadequately prepared for general war. After submitting several memoranda on these lines to Brauchitsch, Beck finally induced him to summon a secret meeting of commanding officers on 4 August 1938. All accepted the validity of Beck's points, but the meeting was allowed to disperse without coming to a positive decision to act.

[16] Ibid., p.54
[17] *Im Hauptquartier*, op. cit., p.31
[18] *IMT*, Vol. XV, p.358

After Hitler had taken steps to restore his authority, there occurred the sensational diplomatic moves culminating in the Munich conference. Because of the infirmity of will shown later by the Generals, it is impossible to assert that, but for Chamberlain, action to restrain Hitler would have been taken. What can be said with confidence is that, after Munich, there was no longer any chance that the Generals would act. In the first place Beck, the only man who had displayed the requisite resolution, had resigned (though this was not announced till November 1938). Secondly, Hitler's achievement in securing the Sudetenland without firing a shot had removed the chief plank, on which the broad-based conspiracy rested, and at the same time consolidated his position in the country as a whole.

Why were the Generals so hesitant at a time when Germany was not yet at war and the spectre of a new abdication and a new 'stab in the back' had not arisen to haunt them? In order to answer this question satisfactorily it is necessary to review briefly the development of strategic thinking in Germany between the wars and some of the controversies that had taken place. In doing so we shall be able to consider the concept of *Blitzkrieg* and Hitler's contribution to it. One important by-product of this was to bring about a division of opinion among senior officers, some of whom aligned themselves with Hitler on mainly professional grounds. In giving these grounds priority they were, of course, remaining faithful in their fashion to the Seeckt tradition of the non-political officer corps. This cleavage, which was also related to the gap between generations, contributed to the failure to present a common front to Hitler, who was quick to exploit the gap, and even widen it, by favours and bribes in the form of gifts of land and even of money.

All German strategists, both professional and amateur, were agreed after the experiences of the First World War, on certain fundamental points. One was that, if possible, a two-front war should be avoided. A second was that Germany must not again become involved in static warfare, which Hitler had described as 'a degenerate form of war'.[19] The very fact that the Treaty of Versailles had forbidden use of tanks and aircraft and insisted on a quota of cavalry in the permitted army of 100,000 men had made the Germans all the more determined to experiment in secret with mobile, mechanized warfare, and some of the last-ditch resistance offered by cavalrymen in Britain was eschewed. Germany's situation 'in the middle of the house' of Europe (as Schlieffen had put it) none the less forced military minds to consider also the need for strong points defended by heavy artillery. For war on one front could hardly be assured and, if war on two fronts developed, it would be necessary to defend one whilst taking the offensive on the other. The West Wall was Hitler's recognition of this, though he constructed no fortified line in the East. His keen politico-military eye was always searching for an opening to use *Blitzkrieg* methods, combined with 'salami' tactics, to isolate and destroy successive enemies in a series of swift blows. This strategy was perfectly designed both to shield Germany from the weakness of her economic and geographical situation and to exploit the 'Maginot' mentality of opposing Generals, who had failed to assimilate the lessons of the First World War. Most German military experts accepted the theory, though few at first shared Hitler's optimism and his low rating of the Anglo-French will to resist.

Differences of opinion emerged, when it came to moving from theory to practice. Beck, like his successor, Halder, was an artillery-man and believed that the barrage and the steady advance of the infantry were the key to victory on the battlefield. He and those who thought like him did not oppose the use of tanks, but held that these should be deployed in support of the infantry. This ran contrary to the ideas of Guderian, who wished to combine motorized troops and armoured vehicles with massed tanks and anti-tank units, in order to make deep penetrations through the enemy lines. The *Panzer* Division

[19] *Hitler Speaks*, op. cit., p.13

48

developed from this concept, which was supported by Blomberg and Reichenau, as well as by younger men, such as Manstein.

Hitler had written in *Mein Kampf* of 'the general motorization of the world, which in the next war will make its appearance in an overwhelming and decisive form'.[20] When he came to power, Guderian demonstrated to him the deployment of *Panzers* and won his approval.[21] Hitler's intervention thus enabled the advocates of *Blitzkrieg* methods to break the stranglehold of the older generation, represented by Beck. It is no coincidence that neither Guderian nor Manstein would have anything to do with the resistance movement, even when it had become clear that Hitler was losing the war. The critical attitude towards Hitler, as military leader, which is exuded by nearly all the memoirs written since the end of the war by his Field-Marshals and Generals, was only adopted with unanimity when it was too late to save Germany and, indeed, to save Europe. The knowledge that some of their colleagues felt more respect for Hitler's talents as war lord than fear of his unbridled ambition seriously deterred the few who, like Beck, believed that he would bring them all alike to ruin.

What assessment can we objectively make of Hitler's abilities as a war leader? That he had great abilities we cannot doubt; but in the list, opposite each plus, there is a corresponding minus sign to be found. As his career passed its zenith, and his active and dynamic side found less and less scope, the minuses became dominant. Whilst it was the year from the failure before Moscow to the fall of Stalingrad that proved decisive, the defects of his qualities were also clearly discernible in the year from the fall of France to the invasion of Russia, and it is appropriate to formulate them here.

It was Hitler's great asset – up to a point – that he viewed the world in terms of ideology which, as a contemporary authority has written, 'gives its adherents a

[20] *Mein Kampf,* op. cit., p.537
[21] *Panzer Leader,* op. cit., p.36

sense of consistency and certainty that is too often absent among those . . . brought up in the tradition of short-range pragmatism'.[22] Unlike the pragmatists, he also had a long-term plan to match his ideology, though he was prepared, as he showed in the summer of 1939, to change dramatically, if he had to, the route by which he aimed to arrive at his goal. In addition, he had complete confidence in his historical mission, believing that, if his will remained inflexible and could dominate the minds of others, his mission was certain to be fulfilled.

The defect of ideological conviction is that the more convinced one is, the less prepared one is to admit the existence of facts that do not fit in – what Kipling called 'the undoctored incident that actually occurred'.[23] The more the ideologue at first succeeds, the less willing he is to accept the non-confirming reality around him, until it suddenly rises and engulfs him. As his loyal General Guderian said of Hitler on the Russian front, he was 'living in a world of fantasy'.[24] He had been reduced to this condition by persistently refusing to accept information that failed to conform to his preconceptions. Thus, as his equally loyal General Manstein said, he 'turned his back on reality'.[25] He 'had little inclination to relate his own calculations to the probable intentions of the enemy, since he was convinced that his will would always triumph in the end'.[26] The fact that his dangerous and onerous mission had to be accomplished in his own lifetime also meant that he was always in a hurry; the skill with which he at first waited for the propitious moment to gain his end began to desert him, as he felt his time growing shorter. As Halder wrote, 'There was no one to follow him, and his work had to be completed during his own short life.'[27]

[22] *Ideology and Power in Soviet Politics:* Z. K. Brezinski (London, 1962), p.5
[23] *'The Benefactors'* in *The Years Between:* R. Kipling (London, 1919)
[24] *Panzer Leader*, op. cit., p.244
[25] *Lost Victories:* E. v. Manstein (Chicago, 1958), p.277
[26] Ibid.
[27] *Hitler as War Lord:* F. Halder (London, 1950), p.2

The obverse of Hitler's confidence in his destiny and
that of the Germanic peoples, whom he led, was his contempt for his adversary, especially if the latter was of
'racially inferior' Slav stock. Up to a point his shrewd eye
for the weaknesses of his foes was an asset; but each time
his judgement of them was confirmed, he was tempted to
accept even greater risks when the next challenge presented itself, until, as Manstein wrote, he was deprived
of 'all sense of judgment regarding what could be
achieved and what could not'.[28] The same excessive self-
reliance and want of sympathy for non-Aryans made him
a bad ally, unable to co-operate with the Italians and
Japanese, or even to give them information about his
plans. The master-slave relationship was the only one
in which he was at ease; exasperated as he was by the
overthrow of Mussolini, it at least enabled him, after the
rescue of the *Duce*, to reduce him to subservience, instead
of the uneasy equality that had previously prevailed.

The concomitant of Hitler's sense of purpose and of
urgency was a dynamism that continually drove him to
take the offensive; the *Blitzkrieg* methods were ideally
devised for this, and proved strikingly successful against
countries smaller than Germany, which tended to collapse
when certain vital nerve centres had been destroyed.
These relatively easy successes, which surprised the
German military experts, as well as those of other
countries, had the effect of inhibiting any serious consideration of the question whether the same methods
would prove equally successful against the vast territory
of Russia, whose reserves and resources were an almost
unknown quantity. Into the aperture created by this
ignorance the pseudo-omniscience of ideology entered
with fatal results. The Russians, Hitler assured Halder,
'lacked any kind of technical ability'.[29] When the invasion
began, it was soon discovered that the Red Army's T34
tank was superior to any in possession of the Germans
at that date. As the first impetus of *Blitzkrieg* spent itself,

[28] *Lost Victories*, op. cit., p.275
[29] *Hitler as War Lord*, op. cit., p.20

the results of Hitler's excessive emphasis on attack began to show themselves: there was no fortified line in the East, to which the German army could withdraw, nor any winter clothing to keep out the Russian winter. Nor was there any strategic reserve. One month before the invasion General Fromm had reported: 'Then in October there will be nothing left, unless on 1st August we call up the 1922 age-group (last reserve).'[30] Hitler was not interested; the war was to be over by then.

Finally, we must take into account Hitler's technical expertise, which was certainly a plus factor in the early years of German rearmament. As Manstein has recorded, Hitler 'possessed an astoundingly retentive memory and an imagination that made him quick to grasp all technical matters and problems of armaments . . .'[31] Albert Speer's judgement is more cautious: 'I still take the view that, with his acquired knowledge in this field, he was indeed able to astonish his military entourage and even alarm them, if they were not as well informed as Hitler himself. But I do not believe that his decisions on the broad issues kept pace with his knowledge of detail. No doubt he had, in fact, influenced "progressively" the development of the *Panzer* and insisted at an early date on the long tank gun; but in other areas he failed, as, for example, over the jet-fighters that he wanted to turn into bombers.'[32] The fact is that even thirty years ago the range and variety of weapon technology made it impossible for any one man, especially if without specialized training, to become equally expert in all fields. In Hitler's case this need not have been disadvantageous if he had been willing to listen to advice; but, here again, his obsession with his own infallibility was ruinous. Signs of this arrogance were in evidence even before his spectacular success in France. Hassell relates how early in April 1940 Krupp spent two and a half hours with Hitler, 'who had spoken only about

[30] *Halder Kriegstagebuch:* ed. H. A. Jacobsen (Stuttgart, 1963), Vol. II, p.422
[31] *Lost Victories*, op. cit., p.274
[32] Letter from Prof. A. Speer to the author of 8 May 1973

production of arms. He (Hitler) is becoming more and more of a universal genius – at least in his own opinion!'[33]

One of Hitler's decisions, which proved to be of vital importance, was much influenced by ideology and ignorance; this was his decision not to give priority to research on atomic weapons. It is true that in June 1942 Heisenberg submitted a discouraging report to Speer, who relayed it to Hitler.[34] Speer himself has recorded, however, that Hitler was also influenced by the Nobel Prize winner Philipp Lenard, who was bitterly opposed to Einstein and regarded nuclear physics as 'Jewish physics'.[35] If Hitler's ignorance in physics requires any proof, this can be found in his favourable reception of Hans Hoerbiger's cosmology of eternal ice,[36] which was also espoused by Himmler.

We can now draw brief, general conclusions about Hitler as war leader. He was a man of ruthless determination and quick, intuitive judgement, with an aptitude for technology and a ready grasp of political and strategic problems. These characteristics put him far ahead of the democratic politicians and petty dictators (Stalin is not here under consideration) with whom he had to deal in the period from 1933 to 1940. But he also had the defects of his qualities and, as his tyranny became more absolute, these defects were fatally exacerbated by his ideological obsessions, which flawed his perceptions and precluded balanced appraisal. By 1940, therefore, his powers of effective decision-making were already on the decline. If we leave moral considerations out of account, we can conclude that in the earlier years, when his senior civil and military advisers were more inclined to oppose him, they were usually wrong in doing so; but in his later years, when opposition had become imperative, Hitler had either rid himself of the malcontents, or cowed them

[33] *The Hassell Diaries* (London, 1948), p.122
[34] *Deutschlands Ruestung im Zweiten Weltkrieg:* W. A. Boelcke (Frankfurt, 1969), p.137
[35] *Inside the Third Reich:* A. Speer (London, 1970), p.228
[36] *Hitler's Table Talk*, op. cit., entries of 21.2.42, 28.4.42 and 25.1.42

into submission. By mid-1940 he stood almost alone; resistance had dwindled to an ineffectual band of conspirators. When defeat once more swelled their ranks and in July 1944 they finally struck, the war had been irretrievably lost.

# IV

## The War Lord in Action

The decisions of the Munich conference together with the fact that these were taken in the absence of Soviet representatives, affirmed Hitler's predominance in Europe; when he asserted his demands, the Chanceries of Europe studied his words with apprehension and tried to assess the limits of his 'patience'. His response to the strong wine of success was, as always, to reach for more, rather than to pause to digest his gains. He was still looking east; the weakness shown by the Anglo-French had encouraged him to move in that direction even if their neutrality could not be assured. During the Munich crisis Poland had not merely observed her Non-Aggression Pact with the Reich, but had succumbed to Hitler's pressure to enrol her as a partner in crime and so acquired from Czechoslovakia the important coal bearing area of Teschen. The Poles did not have long to wait before Hitler offered them a more grandiose and speculative partnership. In October 1938 Hitler proposed extension of the 1934 Pact, if Poland would cede Danzig, grant extra-territorial transit across the Polish 'corridor' and join the Anti-Comintern Pact. This proposal was accompanied by hints of compensation in the Ukraine at Soviet expense. In January 1939 the Polish Foreign Minister, Colonel Beck went to Berchtesgaden and was subjected to Hitler's usual admixture of threats and blandishments. At the end of the same month Ribbentrop paid a return visit to Warsaw; failing to persuade the Poles to co-operate on his terms, he claimed to have said afterwards to his staff, 'Now we must come to an agreement with Russia, unless we want to see ourselves completely encircled.'[1]

The significance of these negotiations, however half-

[1] *The Ribbentrop Memoirs:* ed. A. v. Ribbentrop (London, 1954), p.101

hearted on the Polish side, was not lost upon Stalin: either the Poles and Germans would come to an agreement at his expense or Hitler, confident in the passivity of the Anglo-French, would crush Poland and the Baltic States in one swift blow, bringing the Wehrmacht to the gates of Leningrad. From Stalin's point of view it was essential to weld these interposed states into his defensive glacis, either with the co-operation of the Anglo-French or with the connivance of Hitler. If in the process the latter's hostility could be diverted against the West, Stalin would be able to sit back and feed the flames whilst the capitalist powers destroyed one another. Like Hitler's Generals, Stalin overestimated Anglo-French military strength and believed that the struggle between the democracies and the Fascist powers would be a long and bloody one. On 10 March 1939 he decided to indicate that he was open to an offer; he made a speech at the Eighteenth Party Congress, in which he ascribed to Anglo-French intrigue the diplomatic rumours of Hitler's aggressive designs. When the latter responded by shutting down anti-Soviet propaganda, Stalin took an even more positive step by getting rid of Litvinoff, who was associated with the policy of co-operation with the League of Nations. His successor, Molotov, as one of his first moves, suggested that the economic negotiations, which had been making intermittent progress since the end of January 1939, ought to rest on a 'political basis'.[2]

This accelerated tempo was part of the sequence of events following upon Hitler's occupation of Prague on 15 March 1939 and his declaration of a German Protectorate over Bohemia and Moravia, with Slovakia becoming a client state. He had thus advertised to the world that revision of Versailles was only the first phase of his expansionist policy and that the next phase was already under way. The shock of this belated realization led in London to the impetuous abandonment of the policy consistently pursued since 1919 of declining responsibility

---

[2] *The Incompatible Allies:* G. Hilger & A. Meyer (New York, 1953), p.297

for the frontiers then established on Germany's eastern borders. There has been a tendency to minimize the importance of this reversal of policy, by laying undue stress on the continuing Anglo-German contacts during the summer of 1939.[3] However enthralled we may be by revelations of secret emissaries and the persistence of Horace Wilson and Neville Henderson in the paths of peace, the basic facts remain and cannot be discounted: Britain did give a guarantee to Poland; did attempt to give it substance by an agreement with the USSR and, even when the attempt failed, did declare war. Mistakes, of course, were made; but it was an honest policy, designed, however belatedly, to preserve the independence of smaller European powers. Stalin's choice was to align himself with the Nazi dictator. It was a gamble that for twenty-two months seemed to have paid off; at the end of that time it left him alone on the mainland of Europe, face to face with Hitler, who, partly as a result of Soviet economic help, was stronger than he had been in 1939.

When Hitler received Halder as the army's new Chief of Staff, he said to the General, 'You should take note of one thing from the start, that you will never discover my thoughts and intentions until I am giving my orders.'[4] This advice was strikingly illustrated during the summer of 1939, as it was to be again in the following summer. At the beginning of April, one week after Poland had finally rejected his proposals, he had instructed Keitel to plan the invasion. On 23 May 1939 he received his Service Chiefs and senior staff officers and informed them that, 'further successes could only be achieved by shedding blood'.[5] Poland must be crushed; Britain and France, he believed, would not fight; he added a hint of improved relations with Russia. For the next three months, whilst the OKH worked on the operational plan, they remained under the shadow of the two-front war.

[3] *The Foreign Policy of the Third Reich:* K. Hildebrand (London, 1973), pp.83-8
[4] *Conspiracy against Hitler in the Twilight War:* H. C. Deutsch (Minneapolis, 1968), p.32
[5] *DGFP*, Series D, Vol. VI, p.574

Then on 22 August, before a wider audience of military leaders, Hitler announced his master stroke: Russia would be neutral.

There was a feeling of relief; Anglo-French intervention seemed less likely; also as Field-Marshal Kesselring wrote, referring to the occasion with benefit of hindsight after the war, 'German armed forces were no match for Russia's military might'.[6] Hitler insisted that to win living space was as vital as ever: 'after the defeat of Poland he would fix a new eastern frontier.'[7] That Russia had been conceded her full share in this process remained so obscure to the OKW that, when Koestring telegraphed from Moscow in mid-September that the Red Army was on the move, the cry went up in Berlin, 'Against whom?'[8] What Hitler had omitted to add was that the price he had paid for Russian neutrality, embodied in the secret protocol to the treaty of 23 August 1939, was to consign to the Soviet sphere of interest Finland, the Baltic States and part of Poland, as well as Romanian Bessarabia. This meant that, except for the small gap represented by the Romanian province of North Bukovina, which Stalin seized in the following year, there was now a solid barrier between Hitler and the coveted Ukraine, extending from the Baltic to the Black Sea.

The stroke of policy that relieved the minds of the Generals grieved the ideological wing of the NSDAP. Rosenberg queried in his diary: 'Did the Polish question have to be settled now and in this way?'[9] Darre related to him with disgust how Ribbentrop had found himself quite at home among the Bolsheviks in Moscow – 'as if among old party comrades'.[10] The pact was not merely a denial of everything that the NSDAP had stood for, it had also seriously damaged one of the fundamentals of Nazi foreign policy. Some 500,000 ethnic Germans in the

[6] *Memoirs of Kesselring* (London, 1953), p.44
[7] *DGFP*, Series D, Vol. VII, p.200
[8] *Im Hauptquartier*, op. cit., p.48
[9] *Das politische Tagebuch Rosenbergs*: ed. H. G. Seraphim (Munich, 1964), 25.8.39
[10] Ibid.

Baltic States, Bessarabia and former Polish provinces would either have to be evacuated or left to the tender mercies of the Russians.[11] The Germanic tide that was to have rolled eastward had been turned back. When Hitler received Rosenberg at the end of September, he was – for him – a little on the defensive: 'He had chosen the lesser evil and achieved an immense strategic advantage.'[12] He turned quickly to his plans for creating a reservation in Poland, into which German, as well as Polish, Jews would be driven.

Rosenberg's question remains: why did Hitler think it necessary to break with the past of Nazism in so dramatic a manner, and also incur the criticism directed against him four months later by Mussolini, in order to keep to the timetable he had laid down for the invasion of Poland? Part of the answer, as he himself stressed in addressing his military leaders on 22 August 1939, was that he was a man in a hurry; the programme was arduous and had to be completed in his lifetime.[13] In addition, he was still subject to severe economic pressures, in spite of digesting the spoils of Austria and Czechoslovakia. These could have been relieved, of course, by reducing the proportion of national resources devoted to armaments; but this, too, would have interfered with the timetable. He was equally unwilling to throttle back production for private consumption, which, as a percentage of GNP, fell only by 6% between 1939 and 1940, whilst military expenditure had increased by 15% over the same period.[14] Production of guns and butter on such a scale could only be maintained if the looting went on. Slave labour would also solve Germany's acute manpower shortage.

Finally, it will be recalled that, although in Volume II of *Mein Kampf* Hitler had come out strongly in favour of regarding Britain as his potential ally and Russia as his enemy, in Volume I he had rationally discussed these

---

[11] *RKFDV*, op. cit., p.85
[12] *Tagebuch Rosenbergs*, op. cit., 29.9.39
[13] *DGFP*, Series D, Vol. VII, p.200
[14] *Design for Total War*: B. A. Carroll (Hague, 1968), p.177

alliances as alternatives one to the other.[15] In the long run Britain, unless prepared to co-operate on his terms, would be as much his enemy as Russia; no alliance was more than a temporary expedient. He had intended first to secure hegemony in Europe by defeating Russia; but British recalcitrance had forced him to reverse the sequence. That this was indeed his reasoning is shown by the decision taken at the end of January 1940 to give priority in war production to the Navy.[16] In spite of army and Luftwaffe complaints, this priority was maintained until August 1940 when, as we shall see, Hitler's mind was once more turning to plans for invading the USSR.

Hitler outbid the Anglo-French for Stalin's favour because, in the short-term, it was more important to him. The Anglo-French hoped to restrain Hitler and save Poland by means of a war chariot drawn by two horses in the east – Russia and Poland; if the two horses would not pull together – and this was Poland's decision – the one horse could only be the Polish one. As Halifax and Bonnet, the French Foreign Minister, agreed as early as 21 March 1939, 'It was absolutely essential to get Poland in. Russian help would only be effective if Poland were collaborating.'[17] It was not fully grasped, when the Anglo-French guarantees were given, that with only one horse the chariot could not be drawn at all.

Hitler's position was essentially different. He had no doubt about the capacity of the Wehrmacht to deal with the Polish army, though he may to some extent have shared Stalin's surprise that the war lasted only nineteen days. What concerned him was that Germany should receive an uninterrupted flow of the strategic war materials needed for the fulfilment of his programme. This was assured by the Russo-German economic agreement signed

---

[15] *Mein Kampf*, op. cit., pp.130-1
[16] *Geschichte der deutschen Wehr-und Ruestungswirtschaft:* G. Thomas (Boppard, 1966), p.132
[17] *Documents on British Foreign Policy*, Third Series, Vol. IV, p.425

on 19 August 1939. As the Reich Chief of Naval Operations said in October, 'The importance for us of Russia's economic aid is decisive. Their offer was so generous that the economic blockade is almost bound to fail.'[18] The spectre of 1918 had been banished; as Hitler himself commented, 'We need no longer fear the blockade.'[19] We shall consider in detail in Chapter IX the dependence of the German war effort upon Soviet raw materials; here it is only necessary to add that Stalin not only placed the Soviet railway system at Hitler's disposal to enable the latter to draw supplies, such as rubber, from South East Asia, but that the Russians also circumvented the British blockade by buying metals for Germany in third countries and refusing to give any guarantees against re-export.

One by-product of this Soviet activity was to exacerbate feeling in Britain, which was in any case deeply resentful of the way in which Molotov had handled the negotiations with the rival suitors in Moscow in the summer of 1939. When the Red Army invaded Finland at the end of October 1939, there were cries of outrage in all British newspapers, except the Communist *Daily Worker*. The Foreign Office promoted recruitment of volunteers to fight in Finland, though few of them got there in time. At the end of the year the British Ambassador in Moscow was withdrawn and the post remained vacant for five months. Stalin left Ambassador Maisky in London, but he turned Comintern propaganda loose on the Anglo-French imperialists. When the latter rejected Hitler's spurious peace offer of 6 October 1939, they were accused in Moscow of trying to turn the conflict into a world war. It took Hitler's invasion of Russia to restore a measure of harmony to Anglo-Soviet relations. This point needs to be stressed, because during 1940 Hitler repeatedly used the specious argument with Raeder and those Generals who were opposed to his eastward move that Russia must be eliminated because of her *rapprochement* with Britain, which was giving Churchill increased

18 *The Russo-German Alliance*: A. Rossi (London, 1950), p.110
19 Ibid., p.109n

confidence. Hitler was himself the moving force behind the *rapprochement*, which only began in the summer of 1941.

Hitler had, on the whole, allowed Brauchitsch and Halder to conduct operations in Poland, though he had given a foretaste of things to come by altering plans for the northern Army Group in order to speed up encirclement of Polish forces round Warsaw.[20] If the Generals thought their success in Poland would put them in Hitler's good books, they were soon disillusioned. Certain Generals had tried to take disciplinary action against SS-SD atrocities behind the lines, thus showing their lack of political and ideological insight, which Hitler sought to remedy by afterwards organizing a lecture course for them.[21] When Hitler came to Warsaw for the victory parade, he ignored the hospitality arranged for him by the army commanders and ostentatiously joined the troops at their field kitchens.[22] There is no doubt that Hitler was emotionally identified with front-line soldiers, though not to the extent of wishing to spare their lives if his plans were at stake. In a stormy interview with Brauchitsch early in November 1939 Hitler's rage seemed to be specially stimulated by the Army Commander-in-Chief's suggestion that the troops were not yet battle-hardened. After the Fuehrer's conference of 23 November Brauchitsch offered his resignation.[23]

The principal cause of estrangement, however, was the reaction of the military leaders to Hitler's determination, notified to them before the end of September, to attack in the west in the remaining months of 1939.[24] In Manstein's view, 'the General Staff was eliminated for all practical purposes . . . in the weeks following the Polish campaign'.[25] A recent authority, following Manstein, as-

[20] *Die oberste Wehrmachtfuehrung:* H. Greiner (Wiesbaden, 1951), p.54
[21] *Panzer Leader*, op. cit., p.87
[22] *Lost Victories*, op. cit., p.61
[23] Ibid., p.88
[24] *Oberste Wehrmachtfuehrung*, op. cit., pp.59-67
[25] *Lost Victories*, op. cit., p.71

cribes to incompetence and lack of foresight the failure of
the OKH to have a plan of attack in readiness and their
reluctance to prepare one.[26] They were in no haste to
draft one, because they hoped for peace; if no peace were
concluded, they did not believe Germany should attempt
to breach the Maginot Line and embark on a general
offensive before 1942. General v. Leeb on professional and
moral grounds wished to put a brake on Hitler's aggressive
plans; Generals Rundstedt and v. Bock agreed mainly on
professional grounds.[27] Passive resistance was their only
means of applying the brake, now that the Reich was at
war, without breaching the code of conduct of a lifetime
and abandoning their allegiance to the state. Even
Reichenau and the ambitious General v. Kluge incurred
Hitler's irritation by recommending postponement until
spring 1940.[28] To dismiss all this opposition as due to a
mixture of improvidence and lack of competence is not
only to ignore the moral dilemma, but to make the assumption that a late autumn offensive would have had the
same swift success as that undertaken in the dry spring
of 1940. It is also quite unhistorical to imply that in
1939 every expert should have known that the French
army was as weak as it showed itself to be in 1940; even
shrewd observers like Stalin had staked money on the
French; as he said to Ribbentrop, 'France still had an
army worthy of consideration'.[29]

However that may be, the fact remains that Hitler was
incensed with the General Staff and even less inclined
than before to make them privy to his intentions. He was
certainly not prepared to accept advice from the OKH
after the striking success of the Battle of France had once
more vindicated his judgement and condemned their
pessimism. This latent antagonism between the Fuehrer
and his senior staff officers, most of whom disapproved on
varying grounds of his plans, but repeatedly found them-

[26] *German Strategy against Russia:* B. A. Leach (Oxford, 1973),
pp.38, 45
[27] *Conspiracy against Hitler,* op. cit., p.120
[28] *Oberste Wehrmachtfuehrung,* op. cit., p.65
[29] *DGFP,* Series D, Vol. VII, p.225

selves in the wrong, bred a kind of paralysis where, in the interest of efficiency, free discussion should have reigned. Manstein has summed it up very well: 'Since no one – least of all OKW – was authorized to draft "a war plan", the effect in practice was that everyone left things to "the Fuehrer's intuition". Some, like Keitel and Goering, did so in credulous adulation; others, like Brauchitsch and Raeder, in a mood of resignation.'[30] It should, therefore, occasion no surprise that in the latter part of June 1940, with France prostrate and the British Expeditionary Force evacuated without its equipment, there was no strategic plan in existence for the prosecution of the war, in the event that Churchill refused to admit defeat.

Whilst this remarkable state of affairs was due in large measure, as we have seen, to the mutual lack of confidence prevailing between Hitler and his senior staff officers, it was also inherent in the working of Hitler's own mind. We have referred several times to his master plan to indicate that he had in mind a grand design, which was to be achieved by a series of related moves; but it was not a plan in the sense that these moves had been worked out in any detail. This served to keep each phase secret and give the design, as a whole, a high degree of flexibility. This aspect was illustrated in the summer of 1939, when the main eastward move against Russia had been postponed in favour of settling accounts with the West. The very speed of the triumph over the French army, however, had dislocated the relationship between the strategic plan and the machinery of war production. Whilst operational orders could be redrafted in a matter of days, production lines could not be so rapidly re-adjusted to amphibious warfare, which would have to be waged against Britain, if she refused to yield. Indeed, the amphibious operation successfully undertaken against Norway, whilst in the long term improving the chances of subduing Britain by means of counter-blockade, had in the short term caused losses weakening the effectiveness of the German navy. We shall see in the next chapter

[30] *Lost Victories,* op. cit., p.154

how throughout the summer of 1940 Hitler was increasingly tempted to use against Russia the efficient instrument for land warfare, which was already in his hand, rather than improvise in the less tried and tested field of amphibious warfare.

The Norwegian campaign provides a good illustration of the flexibility of the grand design, of which it did not originally form part. This does not mean, of course, that Denmark and Norway were to be left to their own devices. On the day of the invasion Hitler said to Rosenberg, 'Even as Bismarck's Reich originated out of the year 1866, so the Great German Reich will originate out of this day's work.'[31] What he meant was that in 1940, as in 1866, against Austria, it was necessary, in order to bring about a greater degree of Germanic unity, for the Reich to attack another group of Germanic people – in this case the Danish and Norwegian group. Originally Hitler had not thought this would be necessary; once he had achieved hegemony in Europe, Denmark and Norway could have been reduced to the status of satellites without fighting. During the inactive winter of 1939-40, however, Hitler became increasingly apprehensive that the Anglo-French would be drawn into the Russo-Finnish war in such a way as to imperil his vital supplies of nickel from Petsamo and, possibly, of ball-bearings from Sweden. The nickel evaded the British blockade by travelling south through neutral waters and Hitler's fears were aggravated by the action of the Royal Navy in mid-February in cutting out the *Altmark* in Norwegian territorial waters.

It is significant that, although the OKW was instructed to prepare the Scandinavian invasion plans, Hitler's original decision was not influenced by their advice, but by Raeder and Rosenberg, who were responsible for bringing Quisling into the Fuehrer's presence. In April the OKW was strengthened by the appointment of Jodl to control the operations of the Command Staff and the OKH was excluded from the Scandinavian theatre; General Falkenhorst was put in command under Hitler's

[31] *Tagebuch Rosenbergs*, op. cit., 9.4.40

direct orders.[32] The institutional duality between the two staffs was thus extended to the field of operations. Because Keitel and Jodl were entirely subservient to Hitler, the latter was drawn into the operational direction of war. He had not himself drafted the plan for the western offensive, though in the autumn of 1939 he had rejected the OKH plan and his own thinking coincided closely with that of Manstein, whose plan was adopted. When the offensive in the west began, however, Hitler showed an increasing tendency to intervene in tactics, as when he prevented General v. Kleist's *Panzer* Group from taking Calais.[33] After Hitler's successes in Norway and France, he was, as Jodl wrote after the war, 'no longer willing . . . to listen to military advisers. . . . From that time on he required of them nothing more than the technical support necessary to implement his decisions, and the smooth functioning of the military organization to carry them out.'[34]

The triumph of Hitler and his widespread distribution of honours and Field-Marshals' batons had drastically reduced the number of those still considering some form of resistance. Their failure to take action during the period of the 'phoney war' now confronted them with an acute dilemma: if they continued to serve, they were implicated in the crimes of the regime; if they withdrew, they were condemned, like Beck, to impotence to influence events. In mid-March 1940 it had seemed that matters might be brought to a head by the evil regime of Hans Frank and Himmler in Poland. General Blaskowitz, who was the army commander there, prepared a memorandum about SS atrocities, which was shown by officers of Military Intelligence (*Abwehr*) to disaffected Generals. Blaskowitz was persuaded into a confrontation with Himmler; but when the latter affirmed that he was acting under Hitler's orders, no further steps were taken.[35] The

[32] *Oberste Wehrmachtfuehrung*, op. cit., p.79
[33] Ibid., p.104
[34] *Hitler: Man and Military Leader:* P. E. Schramm (London, 1972), Appendix II
[35] *Hassell Diaries*, op. cit., pp.95, 103

French campaign, which had been fought in accordance with the normal rules of war, and the subsequent occupation, of which the army was at least nominally in charge, eased the Generals' consciences. Though they never acquired much grasp of Nazi ideology, they were able to observe that the French were not to be regarded as sub-humans (*Untermenschen*) and were not to be subjected to the barbarities applied in Poland and later in the USSR.

# V

## Master of Europe

Arriving now at the critical second half of 1940, we may claim to have established certain general propositions relevant in varying degrees to Hitler's decision to invade Russia. First, there was a long tradition of hostility between the Germanic and Slav peoples, marked in the case of the former by feelings of superiority, which Nazi ideology greatly emphasized. In the particular case of senior army officers, however, more than a decade of mutually profitable co-operation with the Red Army had run counter to the traditional, or ideological, feelings of enmity, and Hitler's decision to avert a two-front war by the pact with the USSR had been welcomed. Before Hitler reverted in the summer of 1940 to his long-cherished aim of winning *Lebensraum* in the east, not even his most time-serving staff officers had broached this project, nor made any plans to embark on it. This was due not so much to improvidence as to reluctance to contemplate such an extension of the war.

Secondly, Hitler himself, in addition to his aim to secure *Lebensraum*, had a grand design of conquest, which in the long run was likely to bring him into conflict with the Anglo-Saxon powers. In the summer of 1938 he had been obliged to modify the design in such a way that, after the fall of France, he found himself still at war with Britain, but at peace with the USSR and also dependent on Russian economic co-operation. The headlong speed at which he had arrived at this situation, together with the lack of confidence between him and the General Staff, meant that he was without a specific plan for the prosecution of the war, in the event that he decided to prolong it, or was forced by British intransigence to do so. Whatever decision he now made was likely to be reached after a minimum of consultation with his staff and would be enjoined upon them by the use of whatever arguments might seem calculated to secure the necessary degree of co-operation, regardless of his own real motives.

We shall, indeed, in the pages that follow, find Hitler employing a variety of arguments to justify his decision to invade Russia, including some which are barely consistent with one another, such as that Russia was too weak to resist, or that Russia was planning to attack Germany and ally herself with Britain. At one time he would claim that, to all intents and purposes, Britain had already been defeated and could therefore be ignored, whilst he pursued his aims in the east; at another he would argue that the only way to finish with Britain was to deprive her of her last hope of a European ally by first destroying the USSR. From these contradictory remarks one might conclude either that Hitler was genuinely at a loss, or that, knowing how unwelcome to his Generals his further eastern adventure would be, he deliberately exposed them to his predilection for covering his tracks and confusing those who might wish to bandy words with him. Some traces of confusion have persisted in the minds of historians; but before seeking to disperse these, we must first examine in more detail the problems that Hitler actually faced and the alternative courses of action before him.

When Hitler proclaimed his willingness to offer generous terms to the British, there is no reason to doubt that, in the short term, he intended to do so. With France prostrate at his feet, he had at his disposal ample territory and booty to pay for the war and provide Mussolini with his unearned increment. With Britain once more at peace, the growing interest in the war of the USA would diminish and Hitler would be free either to allow the German people a first taste of the easy life of the master race in Europe or, more likely, to concentrate his efforts and resources for the assault on Russia. This is not to suggest that Hitler, when on 19 July 1940 he demanded that Britain make peace, was offering a genuine partnership in world power. His *Reichstag* speech served two purposes: first, he hoped that it would provoke dissension in Britain, leading to the fall of Churchill;[1] secondly, it was intended to deceive the German home front, which was showing reluctance to face another winter at war.

It is an illusion to suppose that dictators, armed with every instrument of coercion, are indifferent to the popularity of their regimes. This generalization applies with special force to Hitler as war leader, because he recalled so clearly how weakness on the home front had undermined the German effort in the First World War. He had been disappointed by the sombre attitude of the German people on the outbreak of the Second World War, so different from the joyous patriotism of the days of August 1914; he was aware that national satisfaction in the great victories of 1940 had temporarily submerged, but not removed, the deeper longing for peace. Observers were, indeed, astonished at the apathy. William Shirer, the CBS correspondent in Berlin, recorded on 6 June 1940: 'The church bells rang, and all the flags were out today, by order of Hitler, to celebrate the victory of Flanders. There is no real elation over the victory discernible in the people here. No emotion of any kind.'[2] In September 1940 Hassell wrote in his diary: '. . . the German people are getting more and more war weary, and at heart they are indifferent.'[3] The secret SD reports on public morale, which had been stressing the overriding concern about rations, began in the autumn of 1940 to sound a new note of alarm, as the raids of RAF Bomber Command became heavier and more frequent. Public opinion, however inarticulate, was also a factor leading Hitler to dissemble his still unappeased belligerence. He said in an expansive moment to a staff officer in mid-February 1941 that if England were defeated he could not 'inspire the German people to war against Russia; hence Russia must be dealt with first'.[4]

Hitler seems at first to have been puzzled by Churchill's

---

[1] *Totaler Krieg*, op. cit., p.105
[2] *Berlin Diary:* W. Shirer (London, 1941), entry for 6.6.40
[3] *Hassell Diaries*, op. cit., p.140
[4] *Halder KTB*, Vol. II, p.283

determination to fight on; he was an expert at detecting the moral weakness of an opponent, but lacked all appreciation of moral strength. If Britain, at the expense of Poland and France, could be quit of a barely tenable predicament, what was holding her back? None of the Nazi leaders, up to the very end, had any perception of the moral repugnance felt for them by the outside world, nor the complete want of confidence placed in any assurances they might give. Not much was, of course, to be expected from Churchill himself, but Hitler, who suffered, like his entourage, from the illusion that Britain was governed by Scottish Dukes, Irish Marquises and Press Barons of all varieties, assumed that the Prime Minister of 'blood, tears and sweat' could be got rid of without much difficulty. Although Hitler had considered as early as 21 May 1940 the possibility of having to invade Britain, by the middle of the following month the OKW had still carried out 'no preparatory work of any kind'.[5]

Even before the fall of France Hitler was talking about a move against the USSR: Jodl admitted as much in 1943, though at Nuremberg he later thought fit to put back the date by a month.[6] Speer at this time overheard Hitler speaking to Keitel of a possible attack on Russia.[7] We also have the evidence of Rundstedt's Chief of Staff that at the beginning of June Hitler, assuming that Britain would make peace, was ready to 'begin his settling of accounts with Bolshevism'. Rundstedt is reported to have heard this remark with amazement, on the ground that a campaign against the USSR 'could overtax the German forces'.[8] Similar information reached State Secretary Weizsaecker, who relayed it at the end of June to Halder: 'Britain will probably need a further demonstration of our military strength before giving up and leaving our rear

[5] *Operation Sea Lion:* R. Wheatley (Oxford, 1958), p.16
[6] *Nemesis of Power*, op. cit., p.509
[7] *Inside the Third Reich*, op. cit., p.173
[8] *Hitler Confronts England:* W. Ansel (Duke, NC 1960), p.108

free for the east.'⁹ This was disconcerting; Hitler had, of
course, been speaking and writing for fifteen years about
conquering Russian territory, but had not been in a position to do much about it. Now all was changed; Hitler
was master of Europe. Halder decided to investigate
urgently how an attack on the USSR might be mounted
and on 4 July 1940 he had a meeting with General v.
Kuechler, who was to command the troops to be trans-
ferred to the east, his Chief of Staff, General Marcks, and
Colonel Kinzel, who was in charge of Foreign Armies
East.¹⁰ Whatever the future might hold, it was clearly
prudent to reinforce the thin screen of troops which had
been left on Germany's eastern borders. Halder, who
realized that moves against Britain or against the USSR
were equally on the cards, had already talked to the Chief
of Naval Staff about the prospects for an invasion of
Britain.¹¹ Hitler's short-lived decision in mid-June to
release men from the army provides no clue to his intentions, since the armaments industry was crying out for
manpower and in any case the more mobile army of 120
Divisions, which he envisaged, would have been enough
for an attack on Russia, according to the wholly unrealistic estimate of Red Army strength, on which he was
operating (see p.73 below).

As Britain continued to make no response either to
formal overtures or to more oblique approaches, Hitler
and his staff were increasingly concerned to discover the
reason; it seemed to them that Britain must be placing
her hopes on the USSR. This false conclusion strikingly
illustrates the way in which the thinking of both the
Fuehrer and his Generals was dominated by concepts of
land warfare. In fact, the entire hope of Churchill and
the British people was fixed upon Roosevelt and the
American people, who were linked to them by the life-
line of the Royal Navy; the USA had saved the day in
1918 and would do so again. In any case British military

⁹ *Halder KTB*, op. cit., Vol. I, pp.374-5
¹⁰ Ibid., Vol. II, p.8
¹¹ Ibid., p.3

experts had no confidence in the capacity of the Red Army to withstand the Germans; one year later, on the eve of Barbarossa, the Joint Intelligence Committee in London regarded the Soviet High Command as lacking in initiative and the Red Army as having 'much obsolete equipment', badly maintained.[12] The German view, as we shall see, was similar.

After a conference with Hitler on 13 July 1940 Halder recorded the Fuehrer's views on the puzzle posed by British obstinacy: 'He sees, as we do too, the solution to the problem in the hopes England still has of Russia. He thus calculates that he will have to coerce England by force.'[13] It should be carefully noted that, at this stage, it is Britain, not Russia, that is to be coerced, which is consistent with the issue on 16 July of the directive for operation 'Sea Lion' against Britain. Eight days later Hitler received Brauchitsch for a general survey of the possibilities. They began by considering one of the suggestions put forward by Jodl in a memorandum of 30 June 1940, in which he had proposed securing the co-operation of various countries, including the USSR, in prosecuting the war against Britain, which Jodl, like Raeder, regarded at that date as the chief enemy. Then discussion turned to 'the Russian problem' and there follows, in the record made next day by Halder, who was not present, a first sketch of a plan for the invasion of Russia in the autumn of 1940. This part of the record is introduced by the words, 'It has been reported to the Fuehrer . . .' There is no indication from whom Hitler derived the outline plan, nor the hair-raising misinformation upon which it was based. No more than 'four to six weeks' are allowed for the concentration of German forces, amounting to 'eighty to one hundred Divisions'; the estimate of Soviet strength is contained in the bald and misleading statement: 'Russia has fifty to seventy-five good Divisions.'[14] This last point led Halder to annotate the record with a reminder to him-

[12] *The Soviet High Command:* J. Erickson (London, 1962), p.574
[13] *Halder KTB*, Vol. II, p.21
[14] Ibid., p.31

self to check with Kinzel, who indeed produced two days later the following rather more realistic assessment of Soviet strength: 90 rifle Divisions, 23 cavalry Divisions and 28 mechanized Brigades. As for the build-up of forces, Halder later stipulated eight weeks.[15]

It is necessary to study this episode in some detail, since Barry A. Leach in an otherwise impressive work on Barbarossa advances the theory that the Generals anticipated Hitler's wishes in planning the invasion of the USSR and that the outline sketched for Hitler was the work of Brauchitsch who was seeking to curry favour with his Fuehrer. No support for this supposition is to be found in the record of the Hitler-Brauchitsch interview, nor, as Professor Leach admits, in the testimony of surviving Generals, who knew both men.[16] Even if one regards the last-mentioned evidence as collectively prejudiced, there remains the account written by Helmuth Greiner, who kept the War Diary from 1939-43.[17] He backs the view accepted by other reputed historians, namely that the impetuous project for an attack on Russia in 1940 emanated from Hitler himself. If the question be asked from whom he derived his information, if not from Brauchitsch, various plausible answers can be given, of which the most likely is that he had deliberately used his Chief Adjutant, Colonel Schmundt, in order to by-pass the OKH. It is unlikely that Hitler had been advised on this occasion by the OKW, since it was Keitel who dissuaded him from pursuing the idea of an autumn deadline.

In any case, Hitler was capable of arriving at decisions with a minimum of data before him; on this point Warlimont contradicts his former Chief, Jodl, who maintained at Nuremberg that the Fuehrer, like any other Supreme Commander, required for decision-making maps, estimates of relative strength and the like. Warlimont con-

---

[15] *Kriegstagebuch des OKW:* ed. H. A. Jacobsen (Frankfurt, 1965), Vol. I, p.209
[16] *German Strategy against Russia,* op. cit., pp.55-9
[17] *Oberste Wehrmachtfuehrung,* op. cit., pp.116-17, 292

firms, however, that Hitler, in practice, reversed the normal process and 'especially in the case of the attack on Russia . . . allowed himself to be guided predominantly by the obsessive nature of his political concepts, without giving enough weight to the military circumstances'.[18]

The Fuehrer, who had sought in November 1939 to plunge his army prematurely into battle in the west, was acting similarly in 1940. By contrast Brauchitsch, whatever his exact state of mind on 21 July, of which we know nothing, was noted for his taciturnity in Hitler's presence and had repeatedly shown his disinclination to take the initiative. He was by training and disposition a sober staff officer who, if he had decided on a particular occasion to throw caution and reserve to the winds, would at least have consulted Foreign Armies East and provided himself with the latest report on the Red Army. Nor would he in any circumstances have stepped outside his military role and tried to advise Hitler on the political objectives of the attack, which in Halder's record, as in the Fuehrer's remarks ten days later, are described in terms strongly reminiscent of Nazi foreign policy: 'Political aim: Ukrainian Reich. Baltic Confederation. White-Russia – Finland. Baltic "thorn in the flesh".'[19]

It was not until 29 July that Halder instructed Marcks to 'clarify basic thinking for an offensive in the east'.[20] Even if we reject Halder's post-war testimony that, when issuing this order, he was emphatically opposed to the eastern campaign, the instruction to Marcks proves nothing either way. It is the business of a General Staff to have contingency plans, which may, or may not, be one day put into effect. The question whether to attack Russia or Britain was still an open one. What Brauchitsch and Halder thought about it was set down by the latter on 30 July: 'The question whether, if a decision cannot be enforced against England and the danger exists that England allies herself with Russia, we should first wage against

[18] *Im Hauptquartier*, op. cit., p.64
[19] *Halder KTB*, Vol. II, p.31
[20] Ibid., p.41

Russia the ensuing two-front war, must be met with the answer that we should do better to keep friendship with Russia. A visit to Stalin would be advisable . . . We could hit the English decisively in the Mediterranean, drive them out of Asia . . .'[21]

For once the minds of the OKH and OKW were at one; not only did they not want an invasion of Russia in the autumn of 1940, they did not want it at all. But Jodl, as usual, abandoned his opposition as soon as he saw that the Fuehrer's mind was made up, and on 29 July communicated the decision to the OKW staff. Warlimont has recorded that 'Jodl's word had the impact of a stroke of lightning. The bewilderment became, if possible, even greater, as the first questions revealed that it was not proposed first at all costs to conclude the struggle with England, but on the contrary to conquer Russia . . . as the best means of forcing England . . . to make peace.'[22] This argument – the 1812 syndrome – was indeed produced by Hitler at his conference with Raeder, Brauchitsch and senior staff officers on 31 July. It was produced after the departure from the conference of Raeder, a persistent opponent of Barbarossa, who regarded Britain as the chief enemy and wished to attack her in the Mediterranean, a course also advocated at the conference by Brauchitsch. The later part of the discussion, devoted to Russia, came after a dispute between Raeder and OKH about the landing in England; Hitler may well have thought the moment propitious for stressing his alternative proposal, which would mean switching resources to the army to bring it up to a total strength of 180 Divisions, instead of giving Raeder the additional submarines, for which he had been pleading all summer. The Fuehrer, harking back wistfully to his remarks to Brauchitsch ten days earlier, commented that it would be best if the Russian campaign could take place in 1940, but that was not possible, because 'a stand-still in winter would be serious' and five months campaigning would be necessary. He

[21] Ibid., p.45
[22] *Im Hauptquartier*, op. cit., pp.126-7

spoke again of the political objectives in terms very similar to those he had used when speaking to Brauchitsch alone.[23] He attempted to overcome the reluctance of the Generals by an obscure allusion to 'overheard conversations', implying that he had access to intelligence, of which they knew nothing, contradicting the assurances of his Ambassador in Moscow that no Anglo-Soviet *rapprochement* was actually taking place.

Before considering the 1812 syndrome in more detail, we must first follow the development of operation Sea Lion; if Hitler had taken on 31 July an irrevocable decision to destroy Russia, the directive that he issued next day to unleash the Luftwaffe against Britain, as a preliminary to landing, might be regarded as something of a bluff. This is, indeed, the view of most of the German Field-Marshals and Generals, who have lived to tell the tale. Rundstedt, according to his biographer, was told privately by Hitler in July 1940 that 'he did not intend to carry out Sea Lion'.[24] Kesselring, after pointing out that the air offensive of August 1940 was never harmonized with the invasion plans, concludes that an attack 'was never seriously contemplated'.[25] The views of Manstein and Guderian are broadly similar. The real question, however, is not so much whether Hitler wished to bring about the quick submission of Britain as what degree of risk he was willing to incur in order to do so. The timing and scale of the proposed landings required the highest technical competence; Hitler, for once, was at the mercy of his staff and his staff did not agree among themselves. Only one thing was clear to all: unless the Luftwaffe could secure sufficient ascendancy over the RAF to cover the initial landing force and assure its supplies, the risks were too great. By the end of August not only had Fighter Command held their own, but Bomber Command had begun to raid Berlin, thus tempting Goering to divert his

---

[23] *Halder KTB*, Vol. II, p.49
[24] *Rundstedt: The Soldier and the Man:* G. Blumentritt (London, 1952), p.87
[25] *Kesselring Memoirs*, op. cit., p.83

bombers to terror raids on London, which did nothing to further the aims of Sea Lion. By mid-September it was clear to Hitler that British nerves were not going to crack and the precondition for Sea Lion had not been fulfilled. Thereafter the operation remained on the books only as a cover-plan for military training directed against Russia.

The point to be emphasized is that, before the Luftwaffe assault had got fully under way – let alone failed – Hitler had taken certain decisions, indicating his intention to invade Russia whether Sea Lion took place or not. One was to increase the strength of the army, in accordance with the higher estimate of Soviet might produced on 24 July 1940. Corresponding instructions were given informally on 2 August 1940 to the armaments industry and formally confirmed at the end of September.[26] On 9 August the OKW was ordered to make preliminary arrangements in the east for the reception of the great number of troops that would need to be quartered there (*Aufbau Ost*).[27] On 14 August Goering informed General Thomas, who had long been concerned at the strain imposed on arms production by the need to abide by the economic agreement with the USSR, that deliveries were to be maintained only until the spring of 1941.[28] None of these decisions was irrevocable, but, taken together, they form a pattern which by the middle of August is already incompatible with a serious intention to put the destruction of Britain before that of Russia.

The thesis that Moscow was a station on the loop-line to London makes sense only on the twin assumptions that the war in the east would soon be over and that the Fuehrer could then turn with redoubled energy against his main foe, Britain. As we shall see, the first of these assumptions was indeed made; but, if Britain was the main enemy, Hitler was pursuing an indirect approach of a singular kind. It would, in that event, have been more plausible to have adopted the following measures.

[26] *Geschichte der Wehrwirtschaft*, op. cit., p.233
[27] *OKW/KTB*, I, p.18
[28] *Geschichte der Wehrwirtschaft*, op. cit., p.229

First, skilled men should have been released from the army and put to work on the construction of U-boats and long-range aircraft, in order to cut off Britain from her suppliers. The rate of sinkings in October 1940 provided encouragement for this strategy, though Admiral Doenitz estimated that it would not yield decisive results before the end of 1941.[29] As we have seen, Hitler did not adopt this order of priority in production. The Luftwaffe, it is true, continued its bombing; but out of 783 raids in October 1940 no fewer than 333 were directed against London, instead of being concentrated on port installations and shipping all round the coasts of these islands. Bomber production continued to concentrate on medium-range and dive-bombers.[30]

Secondly, Hitler should have adopted the strategy recommended at different times by Raeder, Brauchitsch and Jodl, of attacking British lines of communication through the Mediterranean, supporting the Italians in North Africa and stirring up trouble for Britain in the Arab world, possibly in concert with Vichy. This alternative will be studied in more detail in Chapter VI; it is sufficient here to point out that this course of action would have meant a frank exchange of views and agreement on common policies with Mussolini. This never materialized; indeed Hitler had no meeting with Mussolini between 18 June (Munich) and 4 October 1940 (Brenner). Between these dates Hitler met twice with Ciano, the Italian Foreign Minister, but conversation turned mainly on the carve up of French territory and the Balkan situation and, in any case, there was at all times an almost complete lack of understanding between the two men. Finally, if Hitler had really regarded Britain as his principal enemy, he would have maintained good relations with Stalin, as Brauchitsch and Halder had hoped, ensured for himself an uninterrupted flow of strategic raw materials from Russia and avoided at all costs pushing Stalin into the arms of Churchill. He would, in short, have refrained

29 *Operation Sea Lion*, op. cit., p.138
30 *Geschichte der Wehrwirtschaft*, op. cit., p.132

from creating a new, major theatre of war, except for egging on the Japanese to force a diversion of British resources by attacking her colonial possessions in the Far East and South East Asia.

What evidence is there to support the other argument used at this time by Hitler to convince his Generals of the need to crush the USSR, namely that he must forestall a Russo-British *rapprochement*, which was already emerging? We have seen that he backed this argument by referring to 'overheard conversations' (p.77), without revealing the source of his information. It has been plausibly assumed that this was a reference to intelligence received from the Italians, who were tapping the reports of the new Yugoslav Ambassador in Moscow, Milan Gavrilovic. Gavrilovic, who arrived on 29 June to open diplomatic relations, was not a trained diplomatist but had made his career in political life; he seems to have read too much into Germanophobe remarks made by Molotov and to have assumed that the Moscow mission of Sir Stafford Cripps was showing results.[31] This interpretation of events was rejected by the experienced German Ambassador in Moscow, Friedrich Werner v. der Schulenburg, who was a firm believer in Russo-German co-operation. Hitler, however, was deeply suspicious of career diplomatists and treated Schulenburg with such contempt that as late as the end of April 1941 he told his Ambassador that he did not intend to make war against the USSR.[32] It would therefore be entirely in character for Hitler to have accepted the evidence of the less reliable source in this instance, especially as it fitted into the thesis he wished to advance.

The fact is that Cripps, though hand-picked to appeal to Soviet prejudices, had not been made welcome in Moscow. When in May 1940 the British government submitted his name as a Special Delegate to deal with trade problems, Stalin refused to accept him, unless he

[31] *Hitler's Strategy: The Balkan Clue*: M. v. Creveld (Cambridge, 1973), p.13
[32] *Incompatible Allies*, op. cit., p.328

came as Ambassador. As a result, he did not have a discussion with Stalin until 1 July; yet twelve days later Hitler was evoking the spectre of a Russo-British *rapprochement*.[33] The realities of the situation were very different, as Maisky in London was well placed to observe: 'The negative attitude of the British Government to the entry of the Baltic States into the USSR gave rise to a number of disputes between London and Moscow, which poisoned the atmosphere . . .'[34] An even more serious obstacle to better relations arose from Stalin's participation in the partition of Poland; as late as December 1941, when he had only just brought the German invasion to a halt and was negotiating an alliance with Britain, the problem of the future frontiers of Poland caused difficulty and delay, even in the midst of war. Hitler had no cause to be under any illusion about the coldness of Anglo-Soviet relations, because he had made a solid contribution to this state of affairs by publishing selected extracts from the records of Anglo-French military planning, which had fallen into his hands. These included the proposal debated by the Allies in the spring of 1940 to bombard Soviet oil wells as a means of cutting off Germany from one of her major sources of supply.[35] It is noticeable that after the end of 1940, when the German military machine was committed to Barbarossa, there is no recurrence of talk of the supposed improvement in Anglo-Soviet relations.

Whilst it seems clear that Hitler deliberately exaggerated the danger he claimed to fear, the fact remains that during the summer of 1940 Stalin had markedly strengthened the defensive glacis on his western frontier. The peace concluded in March with Finland, had improved the defences of Leningrad, as had the occupation of the Baltic States in June. At the end of the same month he

[33] *Halder KTB*, II, p.21
[34] *Memoirs of a Soviet Ambassador:* I. Maisky (London, 1967), p.13
[35] *British Foreign Policy in the Second World War:* E. L. Woodward (London, 1962), pp.101-8

had taken Bessarabia from Romania, as foreshadowed in the secret protocol to his agreement with Hitler of 1939, as well as North Bukovina, which had not been mentioned in the protocol. These advances at Romania's expense brought him nearer to that country's oil fields, on which both Axis powers so largely depended. The prospect of a partition of Romania also excited the revisionism of Hungary and Bulgaria, which had both lost territory to Romania after the First World War. Stalin backed these demands, as well as Bulgaria's claims against Greece, and raised once more Russia's perennial request for modification of the Convention governing the Bosphorus. Stalin, through these moves, had not only advanced his frontiers, but was also giving notice that he was not to be ignored in any further carve up in Europe that might be contemplated.

The unstable situation forced the Axis powers to intervene; at the end of August Ribbentrop and Ciano, without consulting the USSR, met in Vienna and imposed on Romania a settlement that gave South Dobrudja to Bulgaria and most of northern Transylvania to Hungary. Hitler then acceded to Romania's request for a guarantee of her truncated territory, to be symbolized by the presence of a German military mission. At the same time Hitler approved delivery of modern equipment to the army of Finland, which had also been subject to renewed Russian pressure.[36] Stalin lost this round of diplomatic manoeuvre, because all the countries that felt themselves threatened – Finland, Romania and Turkey – took immediate steps to improve their relations with the Reich. It should, however, be emphasized that the Russian threat was against three smaller countries, none of which had a common frontier with Germany; the threat was not directed against Germany, except to the extent that, if these countries fell irrevocably into the Soviet orbit, this would increase German dependence upon the USSR for Finnish nickel, Romanian oil and Turkish chrome.

[36] *Hitlers Strategie,* op. cit., p.236

Although in the event Hitler's economic dependence was not increased in this way, one recent authority has referred to 'the menace of Russia, which stood athwart his economic lifelines in Eastern Europe',[37] and has concluded that 'by the summer of 1940 the danger from the East had begun to seem very great indeed'.[38] It is not easy to follow this reasoning. In the summer of the fall of France, when Britain stood alone against Hitler, he was much less at Stalin's mercy than he had been in August 1939, when the Fuehrer sealed his economic dependence upon Russia in a treaty, which his partner had scrupulously observed. The nature of this economic agreement, which was essentially an exchange of Russian raw materials against German industrial products, especially armaments, was such that it created an incentive for Russia to keep the peace, since she was delivering the raw materials, which were readily available and could only be stored with difficulty, against orders for goods which could not be produced and delivered until a future date. Even so, German performance fell so far behind that at the end of March 1940, in order to prevent any interruption of vital supplies, Hitler actually gave instructions that arms deliveries to the USSR should have priority over Wehrmacht deliveries.[39] Despite difficulties, these exchanges proved so profitable to both sides that an extended agreement was concluded on 10 January 1941; at the time of the German invasion six months later Soviet deliveries were ahead of schedule. It is therefore clear that Hitler was not, in fact, under pressure, though there was, of course, the possibility that pressure could be applied. The effect of all trade is to create a degree of interdependence; it does not follow that trade menaces the security of the trading partners; on the contrary it usually leads to increased mutual confidence and improved relations.

If Stalin had preferred to do a deal with Hitler rather than run the risk of being attacked by him in August

[37] *Hitler's War Aims:* N. Rich (London, 1973), p.162
[38] Ibid., p.205
[39] *Geschichte der Wehrwirtschaft,* op. cit., p.229

1939, when he had the chance of help from Britain and France, why should he court the same risk in 1940, when the Red Army stood alone on the European continent against the victorious Wehrmacht? To pose the question is to answer it; indeed Stalin's actions in the six months before Russia was invaded display every anxiety to avoid war. Hitler's estimate of Stalin's intentions was the same; on 9 January 1941 he assured his military chiefs that Stalin 'was a shrewd man; he would not make any open move against Germany . . .'[40] Hitler did not wish to be economically tied to Russia because he did not regard commerce as the true source of a nation's wealth; as we saw in Chapter II, he believed that only more land and more peasants made a nation strong. Moreover his aim ever since he came to power had been to achieve autarky, thus reducing to a minimum the nation's dependence on resources other than its own. He did not invade Russia because she stood athwart the lifelines of his trade, but because he intended to possess for himself the oil of the Caucasus and the wheat of the Ukraine.

[40] *OKW/KTB*, I, p.257

# VI

## The Mediterranean Option:
## The Balkan Imbroglio

We have seen that Hitler's decision in 1939 to court the USSR and risk war with Britain had meant bringing forward that phase of his grand design in which he would challenge the Anglo-Saxon powers, without having first secured hegemony in Europe. His arms production could not be immediately adjusted to this change of plan; even though the USA was not yet in the war, the German Navy and Luftwaffe lacked the resources to break Britain's Atlantic life-line. Her life-line through the Mediterranean, however, was also of great importance to the British war effort; in these closed waters the Luftwaffe could operate effectively and, if the Italian army in North Africa could deprive the Royal Navy of Alexandria, the Suez Canal could be barred to British shipping. Apart from the dubious attitude of the Egyptians, elements unfriendly to Britain were at work at both ends of the Mediterranean. Franco might be tempted to seize Gibraltar and thus express in a practical way his gratitude for Axis help during the Spanish Civil War. In Syria traditional French mistrust of British policy in the Near East had been aggravated by the bitterness of defeat and the assault of the Royal Navy on the French fleet at Oran. The Mufti of Jerusalem, Haj Amin, was not the only leader in the Arab world hostile to Britain.

In the first week of August 1940 these various possibilities were being actively considered by the OKW, with the full encouragement of Brauchitsch, as a means of pursuing the struggle against Britain during the coming winter, in the event that operation Sea Lion did not take place.[1] On 14 August, whilst Hitler authorized the OKW to undertake an operational study of the seizure of Gibraltar, Jodl discussed with his staff the means of giv-

[1] *OKW/KTB*, Vol. I, pp.5-11

ing German help, if Italy required it, in taking Egypt, and also the need to divert Italian thoughts from irrelevant side-shows at the expense of Yugoslavia. 'Very much closer co-operation than hitherto between the Axis powers would be necessary,' he concluded.[2] But of this there was no immediate prospect. It was precluded by Mussolini's baffled determination to be regarded as an equal and independent partner, and Hitler's decision to respect his fellow dictator's wishes, in order to prevent undermining the latter's prestige at home and abroad. Hitler was well aware of the weaknesses of Fascism; whatever his own complaints against his Generals, they at least could not look to royal protection; he had in the Reich a few contumacious Bishops, but no Pope. Hitler, above all, allowed Mussolini to go his own way, because he, Hitler, was determined not to be deflected in any degree from following his, as a result of having entered into a prior commitment, or accepted an obligation to consult his ally.

The Pact of Steel, therefore, was not, like the Anglo-American alliance, based on an intention to make all important moves in common, but on a delimitation of spheres of separate activity; if Hitler was not prepared to consult Mussolini about his treatment of Poland, or his invasion of Russia, the corollary was his recognition of the Mediterranean as an Italian '*mare nostrum*'. Mussolini and his army were at one in their determination to keep German interference to a minimum; it was only their dismal record of failure, both in North Africa and in Greece, that opened the door. From the beginning Hitler had had it in mind to give the Italians some assistance; when he saw Ciano on 8 July 1940, he stressed the importance of Gibraltar and, after Ciano in grandiose terms announced that an attack on Egypt was imminent, Hitler offered long-distance bombers, which could lay mines in the approaches to the Suez Canal, so long as it remained in British hands.[3] Ciano's response was to turn the con-

[2] Ibid., p.31
[3] *Staatsmaenner u. Diplomaten bei Hitler:* ed. A. Hillgruber (Munich, 1969), p.84

versation to the impertinences of the Greeks, with whom we shall concern ourselves shortly. The Italians were anxious to obtain armoured vehicles, anti-tank guns and other war material from Germany; but the Wehrmacht, itself short of equipment and dubious about its effective use in Italian hands, preferred to send troops. On 5 September the OKW informed the Italian Military Attache in Berlin, who had renewed his request for equipment, that the Fuehrer was prepared to send Panzer units to Libya.[4] The wisdom of this offer became apparent 12 days later, when the Italian offensive ground to a halt after covering little more than 55 miles of desert. Even so, when Hitler repeated his offer of help at his meeting with Mussolini on the Brenner at the beginning of October 1940, the latter at first restricted his acquiescence to the final phase of the forthcoming campaign, namely the assault on Alexandria, though shortly after German preparations to send *Panzer* units began.[5]

This confident Italian attitude had to be abandoned in the face of the British counter-offensive in North Africa, which began on 9 December 1940, and the even more humiliating defeat at the hands of the Greeks. By mid-February 1941 Rommel and his *Afrikakorps*, consisting at first of one light armoured Division, was ready to turn the tide in North Africa, showing how much might have been accomplished if carefully concerted Italo-German plans had been made in good time and, on the German side, carried into effect with more imposing forces. As it was, Hitler's rejection of the OKW recommendation to take Malta, instead of Crete, added to the continuing difficulty in keeping Rommel adequately supplied across the Mediterranean. As Kesselring observed after the war, Hitler 'disastrously underrated the Mediterranean's importance'.[6] When oportunity knocked, Hitler, who hitherto had displayed strategic opportunism of a high order, had his eyes so firmly fixed on the east that he was no

4 *OKW/KTB*, Vol. I, p.64
5 Ibid., p.115; *Staatsmaenner*, op. cit., p.119
6 *Kesselring*, op. cit., p.87

longer willing to be flexible at the risk of having to modify plans for his campaign against Russia.

At the western end of the Mediterranean Hitler had even less to show for his preparatory diplomatic work. Shortly before he imposed the armistice on France he had received indications that Franco might be willing to enter the war, in return for heavy bribes in the form of economic and military aid and large segments of French territory in North and West Africa. Hitler, already saddled with the need to satisfy one 'Johnny-come-lately' in the person of the *Duce*, did not at once add the *Caudillo* to his list; but by mid-August, with Britain still resisting and the difficulties of Sea Lion becoming more and more apparent, Hitler instructed the OKW to make a detailed study of the seizure of the Rock of Gibraltar, on the assumption that he would be able to secure Franco's co-operation.[7] The factor of British resistance, however, which led Hitler to embark on operation Felix, as it came to be called, led Franco to raise his price to a prohibitive level; his Atlantic islands, as well as his Cantabrian coast and overseas trade, were dangerously exposed to the depredations of a maritime power and, in any case, he had never intended to do more than help to carry away the defunct British corpse.

By 17 September 1940, when his Minister of the Interior, Serrano Suñer, visited Hitler in Berlin, the delay in launching operation Sea Lion was already becoming ominous; Suñer indicated that French Morocco and part of Algeria and the French Cameroons would no longer be enough; a correction of the Pyrenean frontier at the expense of France would also be necessary.[8] Hitler made one further effort to persuade Franco to come into line at a modest price that would not drive the French African colonies into the arms of de Gaulle. He travelled on 23 October 1940 to Hendaye, the extreme limit of his conquered territory, in order to confer with Franco, but

[7] *OKW/KTB*, Vol. I, p.32
[8] *Staatsmaenner*, op. cit., p.102

without success. By the end of the year Felix had been written off; as the Fuehrer observed with unusual candour, 'The resolution of the conflicting interests of France, Italy and Spain in Africa is only possible through a grandiose fraud.'[9]

Would one be justified in concluding, as some historians have done, that by this time Hitler had virtually exhausted the possibilities open to him, so that the invasion of Russia was, indeed, the only way in which he could continue to prosecute the war? Was he obliged to create a new theatre of war in the East, because he could do nothing more in the West? These questions can best be answered at this stage by looking at Franco-German relations, which then, as since, supplied the key to co-operation in Europe. On the day after Hitler's abortive meeting with Franco, he met Pétain, with Laval, at Montoire. After assuring Pétain that the outcome of the war 'in a military sense had already been decided', Hitler voiced the opinion that 'for the war to continue any longer would not only be in the first place a burden for Germany, but would also be greatly to the disadvantage of Europe as a whole'.[10] This was the language that the French leaders had hoped to hear, because it seemed to imply collaboration between France and Germany on honourable terms, with the possibility of a peace treaty sooner rather than later. In the autumn of 1940, before de Gaulle offered solid hopes of the resurrection of France 'over the water', and whilst Hitler was at peace with Stalin, neither the far Right nor the far Left in France was in the least worried that collaboration with Hitler meant collaboration against Britain. The agony of France was being prolonged by the stubborn British, who refused to read the logic of events and agree to share with France the heavy price that Hitler and his allies would exact for a lost war.

On 30 October 1940 Pétain announced to the French people that he had accepted the principle of collaboration with Germany, the modalities of which remained to be

[9] *Halder/KTB*, II, op. cit., p.124
[10] *Staatsmaenner*, op. cit., p.145

explored.[11] There matters rested for over six months, inhibiting the reconstruction of Europe, contributing to Laval's fall from power and investing the very word 'collaboration' with the pejorative connotation it bears to this day.[12] Collaboration was as much a semantic casualty of Montoire as 'appeasement' was of Munich. Competent diplomatic observers believed this need not have been so. Hassell wrote in his diary, 'The fall of Laval has demolished all budding hopes for a final agreement. It is the unanimous opinion of the French that Laval . . . would have got France behind him if he had not come with empty hands. If we had given him a few hundred thousand prisoners of war and promised gradually to withdraw the demarcation line (instead of evicting the Lorrainers), he would have been hailed as a saviour. To the public at large Laval is washed up, a traitor in the pay of Germany.'[13] Even Mussolini, though he was not renouncing his pound of flesh, recommended to Hitler at the Brenner that 'the one precondition for French participation in a continental coalition (i.e. against Britain) was the early conclusion of a peace treaty' with France.[14] Hitler replied that he needed French bases for U-boat and Luftwaffe operations against Britain.

This was true enough, as far as it went; but it would have been more honest if Hitler had said that he had no intention of going over to a defensive strategy, permitting European reconstruction, until he had first settled accounts with Russia. Nevertheless, to have adopted the *Duce*'s suggestion would have increased British isolation, by making American intervention less likely, and generated real pressure on Britain to make peace. None of this ever entered into Hitler's calculations, because he had no plan for the reconstruction of Europe, which would have involved some measure of genuine co-operation between Germany and the subject and satellite peoples. 'The New

[11] *Histoire de Vichy:* R. Aron (Paris 1954), pp.309-10
[12] *Das Jahr 1941 in der europaeischen Politik:* ed. K. Bosl (Munich, 1972), pp.143-6
[13] *Hassell Diaries*, op. cit., p.155
[14] *Staatsmaenner*, op. cit., p.117

Order' in Europe was no more than a slogan, masking the reality of the Great German Reich, in which the orders of the master race were to be obeyed without question. This was the only form of co-operation that Hitler understood. The delays and compromises inherent in negotiated agreements between sovereign states were incompatible with the invasion of Russia in the spring of 1941. For this great task Hitler needed French manpower and the produce of French fields and factories, as much as he needed captured French military equipment, without which his eastern offensive could not have been launched on time. At the end of October 1940 Laval observed, 'The Fuehrer is a great man because he has understood that he cannot make Europe without France.'[15] Laval was mistaken: the New Order in Europe was nothing more than the exploitation of the conquered for the purpose of fresh conquest.

A further chance of Franco-German co-operation arose in mid-April 1941, as a result of the anti-British revolt in Iraq and Rashid Ali's appeal to Hitler. When Admiral Darlan went to see Hitler on 11 May 1941, he had already agreed to give facilities at an air base in Syria to enable Rashid Ali's appeal to be met.[16] To have exploited this would have fitted in with projects for a thrust through Syria against British positions in the Middle East, which the OKH and OKW had been nurturing since October 1940; but Hitler ruled that this could only be undertaken after Russia had been crushed.[17] He gave only token support to Rashid Ali, whose revolt soon collapsed. By mid-July Syria, too, was under British control. Hitler rejected proposals to attack Britain in the eastern Mediterranean, which were also advocated by Raeder, on the ground that he would be exposing his flank to the Russians, who must, therefore, first be defeated. However, as we have seen, Stalin, far from seeking an opening to attack, was showing increasing submissiveness, as Barbarossa became im-

[15] *Histoire de Vichy,* op. cit., p.312
[16] Ibid., pp.428-30
[17] *Hitlers Strategie,* op. cit., p.476

minent. Hitler's argument merely provides another example of his refusal to take into account alternatives which would oblige him to change his anti-Soviet plans.

We must now consider another instance of Hitler's ambiguous relationship with Mussolini, namely the latter's 'parallel war' against Greece, which led to increased German involvement in the Balkans and thus aggravated Russo-German mistrust. When Ciano saw Hitler on 8 July 1940, he remarked that 'Italy was very dissatisfied with Greece'; it might be necessary to seize Corfu; he also abused the Yugoslav regime.[18] Hitler, in his reply, made no reference to Greece, which had accepted a British guarantee in 1939 and might be regarded as an object of legitimate hostility; but he warned explicitly against an attack on Yugoslavia, which might encourage Russia to fish in troubled Balkan waters and provide some common ground for a Soviet-British *rapprochement*. Hitler and Ciano met again at the end of August 1940, in the shadow of the tension between Romania and Hungary, and Hitler again insisted that conflict in the Balkans must be avoided.[19] He had good reason to take this stand; Germany imported from South-East Europe half of her total requirements of cereals and livestock.[20] The dependence of the Reich on this area for metals was equally striking; from Yugoslavia and Greece together over 45% of Germany's aluminium needs; from Yugoslavia alone 90% of Germany's tin, 40% of her lead, 10% of her copper, as well as substantial quantities of antimony and bauxite.[21] That Hitler seemed to prefer trade in these commodities to conquest – at least until the end of 1940 – does not contradict the argument used at the end of the preceding chapter in relation to his trade with the USSR; Yugoslavia, like Hungary, was living within the field of Germany's economic predominance and might be expected in due course to assume gracefully the role of a client

[18] *Staatsmaenner*, op. cit., p.85
[19] Ibid., pp.90-2
[20] *Hitler's War Aims*, op. cit., p.182
[21] *Balkan Clue*, op. cit., p.4

state. As we shall see, her ultimate refusal to do so enraged Hitler and brought down his terrible vengeance upon Belgrade. This came as no surprise to the OKH, who in the autumn of 1940 had prepared contingency plans for invading Yugoslavia.[22] At that time, however, Hitler was beginning to concentrate his attention on Barbarossa; he did not wish prematurely to excite Russia's traditional interest in the Slav peoples of South-East Europe.

There can be no doubt that the Germans were aware of the existence of Italian plans directed against Greece, if only because they were able to read Italian cyphers; but the Germans may have assumed that these plans would be designed to stave off any British action in fulfilment of the 1939 guarantee.[23] Indeed Ciano had assured Ribbentrop in mid-August that, 'if the English proceed to occupy some naval bases on the Greek coast . . . we shall have at hand all the military means suitable to prevent such a British action'.[24] The opportunity to clarify these intentions at the Brenner meeting on 4 October 1940 was missed; Mussolini said nothing about Greece, although his invasion was at that time due to begin within 14 days; Hitler said nothing about the despatch of his military mission to Romania, let alone his plans for Barbarossa. On the contrary he went out of his way to assure the *Duce* that 'Russia would not try anything'.[25] The conversation then turned to the problem of reconciling Spanish demands on French territory with French collaboration against Britain, which motivated the Fuehrer's forthcoming journeys to Montoire and Hendaye.

So much for the German official record of the Brenner meeting; but both Raeder and Jodl[26] made the assumption shortly before the invasion of Greece began on 28 October that Hitler had been told what Mussolini was going to do.

[22] Ibid., p.145
[23] *Halder KTB*, Vol. II, p.249
[24] *Balkan Clue*, op. cit., p.19
[25] *Staatsmaenner*, op. cit., p.208
[26] *OKW/KTB*, I, p.124

Even if the assumption was mistaken, recent research has established that Hitler knew by the time he left Berlin on 20 October and decided not to intervene.[27] On his journey he was kept informed of developments, which included a Luftwaffe report that the invasion would begin on October 25 or 26 and would have as its immediate objective the principal Ionian islands, with Salonika next.[28] These would, in fact, have been the logical objectives if the Italians, as they had claimed, were primarily concerned with forestalling the British. By 25 October Hitler certainly knew the correct date, which left him two days for an appeal to Mussolini to change his mind; but Hitler still did not intervene, nor did he speed up his journey to the rendezvous at Florence. Indeed he spent 24 hours in Munich en route, arriving in Florence on the day on which the invasion had begun.[29] When he met the *Duce*, he uttered no reproaches, but offered help in seizing Crete, before the British could land there. Mussolini passed over this offer in silence.

Given this sequence of events, one must ask oneself why Hitler, as early as 1 November 1940, told his staff that his judgement of the Italian operation was 'in every respect negative' and that he was so little in agreement with it 'that he had lost all inclination for close military co-operation with Italy'.[30] Jodl concluded from this remark that the despatch of German *Panzer* units to Libya was now in doubt, in which case a thrust to the Aegean from Bulgaria might be substituted. Although at this stage the Italians were not admitting that things had gone wrong, they made it clear that their immediate objective was in Epirus, implying an extension of their Albanian province, and that it was uncertain whether they would move on Salonika at all.[31] This made it plain that Mussolini was more concerned with expanding his empire at Greek

[27] *Balkan Clue*, op. cit., pp.40-3
[28] *OKW/KTB*, I, p.123
[29] *Balkan Clue*, op. cit., pp.44-7
[30] *OKW/KTB*, I, p.144
[31] Ibid., p.143

expense than with aiming a stroke against Britain; but the price of his vainglory, which both Axis partners might be called upon to pay, was that the British, who on 29 October had begun to land in Crete, would also support the Greeks in Salonika, in fulfilment of their guarantee, and from there threaten the Romanian oil wells. It had no doubt also become clear that the Italians had put inadequate forces in the field, even for their own limited purposes. This impression would have been confirmed, when on 4 November 1940 General v. Thoma, on return from a visit to Libya, presented to Hitler a depressing report on the military incapacity of the Italian army.[32] The OKH was instructed to look into the possibilities of seizing Greek Thrace and Macedonia, if the concurrence of Italy and Bulgaria was forthcoming.

Hitler was usually conscious of First World War parallels and his conversations at this time show great apprehension about the danger of a hostile expeditionary force in Salonika; quite apart from the threat to the Ploesti oil wells, such a force on his flank could imperil his advance into Russia. Only a prompt submission by Greece, or spectacular success for Italian arms, could avert this danger. Since it very soon became evident that neither of these eventualities had occurred, Hitler was not going to admit to his military staff, with whom his reputation as an infallible strategist was at stake, that this awkward situation had arisen through his failure to explore Mussolini's mind and tie him down to a project that would serve the common war effort. It was preferable for Hitler to insist that he had been surprised, thus throwing the blame on his fellow dictator and on liaison officers who, allegedly, had failed to keep him informed. He thus created a legend that for long deceived historians, providing an object lesson in the perils of taking all his words at their face value. By the end of the lost war Hitler had completely convinced himself that it had all been Mussolini's fault; as he said in February 1945, 'We were

[32] Ibid., pp.149-50

obliged against our will to intervene with arms in the events in the Balkans, from which followed inevitably the disastrous delay of our build-up against Russia.'[33]

German strategic thinking was summed up on 12 November 1940 in Directive No. 18, which gave prominence to co-operation with France as a non-belligerent, especially in relation to the French African colonies, and also alluded to the role of the reluctant Spaniards in helping to close the western end of the Mediterranean. The hope was expressed that the Italians would soon advance in North Africa, whereupon the Germans must be prepared, 'if necessary, to occupy from Bulgaria the Greek mainland north of the Aegean Sea'. Finally, the Directive included a guarded reference to Barbarossa (the code-name had not yet been assigned): 'all preparations for the east, for which verbal orders have already been given, will be continued.'[34] Only the last two projects were to reach fulfilment; by the end of the year Laval had fallen from power; Franco was recalcitrant; Mussolini's ventures in Greece and North Africa had come to grief. Italy had ceased to count as a major ally and the problem of keeping her in the war was to weigh more and more heavily upon the Wehrmacht. Hitler was quick to perceive this, but it did not lead him, as it might well have done, to concentrate his efforts on the Mediterranean theatre; if anything, it seems to have increased his determination to open up his own new theatre of war in the east.

The 'parallel war' also had the effect of aggravating the tension between the Reich and the USSR, which had manifested itself since July, and making less likely the adherence of the latter to the Three Power Pact (with which we shall deal in the next chapter). In mid-September reports had reached Berlin that Marshal Antonescu, the new dictator of Romania, felt himself threatened by the USSR.[35] His fears may well have been

[33] *Hitler: Reden v. Proklamationen:* ed. M. Domarus (Neustadt, 1962), Vol. II, p.2205
[34] *Hitler's War Directives:* ed. H. Trevor-Roper (London, 1964), pp.40-3
[35] *OKW/KTB*, I, p.81

exaggerated, but by November 1940 the German military mission in Romania was itself reporting Soviet troop concentrations in Bessarabia and North Bukovina.[36] Hitler's anxiety about Salonika had inevitably increased his interest in Bulgaria and also in Yugoslavia, since the concentration of the Wehrmacht in the former country could best be accomplished by transit through the latter. Both countries were increasingly exposed to the rival solicitations of Hitler and Stalin. The only beneficiary was Turkey, whose chances of remaining neutral improved as German-Russian relations deteriorated.

After the war Jodl wrote of this period: 'The spectre of a massive concentration of forces on the eastern borders of Germany and Romania had taken concrete form, and Hitler was weighing the thought of preventive war. The world has learned from the Nuremberg Trial of many voices that warned against this march. All agree that it was definitely Hitler's idea originally . . . the danger from the east was seen by all soldiers and Hitler's concern was shared, more by some, less by others. Opinions differed whether the danger was really so acute and whether it might not have been possible to deal with it by political means . . .'[37] The one attempt to seek a political solution was represented by Ribbentrop's letter of 13 October 1940 to Stalin and Molotov's visit in the following month to Berlin. This diplomatic move resulted from the efforts of certain of Hitler's advisers, both civil and military, to avert war against the USSR by enrolling her in a common effort to defeat Britain and parcel out among the victors Britain's possessions and areas of interest. It was also an attempt to use Japan to hold the USA in check, whilst this reallocation of world power was taking place; it thus marks the end of the purely European phase of the war. These developments we shall discuss in the next chapter.

[36] *Oberste Wehrmachtfuehrung*, op. cit., p.339
[37] *Hitler: Man and Military Leader*, op. cit., App. II

# VII

## The Continental Bloc: The Three Power Pact

Because the Nazis were more successful in practising genocide against Slavs and Semites, it is easy to overlook the fact that their ideology preached against all non-Aryan peoples, not least those who had already in the Second Reich been subsumed in the slogan 'the yellow peril'. It was, however, a peril more remote than that presented by Slavs, and Hitler recorded in *Mein Kampf* that, for this reason, he had been pro-Japanese at the time of the Russo-Japanese War of 1904.[1] Elsewhere in the book he writes slightingly of Japanese culture and criticizes Britain, who 'eagerly reaches out her hand to a member of the yellow race and enters into an alliance which, from the racial point of view, is perhaps unpardonable . . .'[2] Nevertheless this critical expression sums up in round terms the course pursued by Hitler himself after he came to power. Just as the alienation of the USSR and the 1934 pact with Poland meant a reversal of Weimar European policy, so in the Far East friendship with Japan led eventually to ending the 'special relationship' with China, which had been cultivated by Reichswehr and Foreign Office under the Republic.

Nazi hearts began to warm to the Japanese after both countries had left the League of Nations. Rosenberg, who had had some harsh things to say in the past about 'the yellow peril', described the Japanese state in 1935 as 'admirable for its religious unity, state discipline and its stamp of national sacrifice'.[3] In the same year the Seventh World Congress of the Communist International (Comintern), meeting in Moscow, denounced 'the war

[1] *Mein Kampf*, op. cit., p.143
[2] Ibid., p.520
[3] *Germany and Japan*: E. L. Presseisen (The Hague, 1958), p.8

provocations of German fascists and Japanese militarists'.[4]
A riposte was initiated by Ribbentrop, who was looking
for a chance for his Bureau to distinguish itself in the
field of foreign affairs. He approached Major-General
Hiroshi Oshima, a noted Germanophile, who had become
Military Attache in Berlin, and from this beginning
emerged in November 1936 the Anti-Comintern Pact.
Ostensibly the Pact was not directed against the USSR,
but against the Comintern, thus taking at face value repeated statements of the Soviet government that it was
not to be identified with the international organization.
None the less the Pact was an obvious warning to the
USSR, which in the west had allied herself with France
and Czechoslovakia and in the east had announced her
intention of defending Outer Mongolia against any
Japanese encroachment. The Pact also had a secret protocol, of which the Russians were well aware through
their German agent, Richard Sorge,[5] committing each
party not to conclude a political treaty with the USSR
without the consent of the other; the protocol was destined to be ignored. In 1937, on the anniversary of the
signing of the Pact, Italy adhered to it.

The Japanese attack upon China in 1937 obliged the
German army, to its regret, to bring to an end its long
tradition of providing military advisers to the Chinese
army; but there was a retired General in Bavaria, Karl
Haushofer, who welcomed the prospect of closer relations
with Japan. Haushofer had been a military observer in
Japan before the First World War and had become
strongly Japanophile. After the war he had begun to
lecture at Munich University on the new military science
of geopolitics and numbered Rudolf Hess among his
students. Through this channel he is thought by some
historians to have exerted an influence on Hitler and the
NSDAP. Haushofer certainly addressed in June 1924 a
meeting sponsored by the Nazis and other nationalist
organizations on the subject of geopolitics; but at that

[4] Ibid., p.81
[5] Ibid., p.112

date Hitler was in prison.[6] Haushofer shared with the Nazis a belief in Social Darwinism, which led him to classify the major powers into two main groups: those which were clinging to power after their day was done (*Maechte der Beharrung*), and those destined to inherit the power of the former (*Maechte der Erneuerung*). The first group included Britain and Haushofer wrote of 'the flagging English will to empire'.[7] The USA, which was sustaining Britain, came into the same category. The second group, besides Germany, included both Russia and Japan, who had legitimate claims 'against owners of great spaces, who have not the capacity to develop them'.[8] A great continental bloc of these three countries, using internal lines of communication, could hold its own against the French and Anglo-Saxon maritime powers. Japan's involvement in Manchuria after 1931 had led her in the wrong direction, since she would have done better to turn south and liberate her fellow Asiatics from colonial domination; but there was always hope that, under German influence, wisdom would prevail.

These geopolitical theories evidently had points in common with Nazi policy, including the concept of *Lebensraum*, which was in any case no novelty, having been espoused by the Pan-German League at the turn of the century;[9] but it had nothing in common with race policy, which was the distinctive mark of Nazism. It seems unlikely, therefore, that Haushofer exerted influence on Hitler; in any case by the end of 1938 he was out of favour, though still supported by Hess. It does seem plausible, however, that Ribbentrop, who was barren of political originality, derived from Haushofer the idea of the continental bloc, which he recommended to Hitler in the second half of 1940, as a means of preserving the pact with Moscow, which the Foreign Minister regarded as his

[6] *NSDAP Hauptarchiv*, Microfilm reel 42, folder 857
[7] *Germany's Revolution of Destruction:* H. Rauschning (London, 1939), p.203
[8] Ibid., p.198
[9] *Der Terminus 'Lebensraum':* K. Lange in *VfZg*, Munich, 1965

great achievement, and redirecting the main effort against Britain. When Ribbentrop was setting up his Bureau, before his assignment to London, he had had contact with Haushofer's Geopolitical Institute in Munich and the latter's son, Albrecht, at one time worked for the Bureau.

In March 1934, when Colonel Eugen Ott, who later became Ambassador to Tokio, was received by Hitler, before taking up his post as Military Attache there, he expressed the view that 'distances were too great in Russia for a Far Eastern war to have an influence on the European situation'.[10] The Fuehrer disagreed, though seven years later he was to act, and with grave results, as if he had been converted to Ott's point of view. The Japanese-German friendship was certainly born of common antagonism to the USSR; but after 1938, when Ribbentrop had become Foreign Minister and added his Anglophobia to Hitler's mounting exasperation with British policies, the feeling grew in Berlin that, if Japanese dynamism could be directed southward, it would impose new strains upon Britain, whose interest in Eastern Europe was proving so inconvenient. Oshima, who returned to Berlin as Ambassador in October 1938, proposed to Ribbentrop that the Anti-Comintern Pact might be converted into an open alliance against the USSR.[11] Negotiations dragged, however, and by the summer of 1939, whilst undeclared war between the USSR and Japan had erupted on the Manchurian-Mongolian border, the Germans were covertly negotiating an agreement in Moscow. The Japanese, who in July and August suffered severe military setbacks at Russian hands, were about to meet the fate of all those who put their trust in the Fuehrer.

The pact signed by Ribbentrop in Moscow in August 1939 was a serious blow to Japan, since Article 4 precluded each party from joining 'any group of powers which directly or indirectly is directed against the other party'. In the middle of the following month the Japanese

[10] *Germany and Japan*, op. cit., p.68
[11] Ibid., p.193

came to an agreement with Russia to end the fighting and in October 1939 the unhappy Oshima was withdrawn from Berlin. Tokio declared 'non-involvement' in the war in Europe. For Ribbentrop the situation was embarrassing and this presumably motivated the suggestion he put to Stalin at the end of September 1939 that Japan be invited to co-operate with the new Nazi-Communist partnership. Stalin agreed that this would have the advantage of containing 'England, France and the USA, the satiated nations', but the proposition was not pursued at that time.[12] It was to play a significant role one year later, when Heinrich Stahmer, a former member of the Ribbentrop Bureau, was sent as Special Envoy to Tokio with instructions to join Ott in negotiating some resuscitation of the defunct Anti-Comintern Pact to meet the new situation created by Hitler's defeat of France and the Netherlands, whose colonies tempted Japanese ambition, his changed relationship to the USSR, the continued resistance of Britain and the increasing support granted to her by the USA. Italy was to be a member of the new pact, as of the former one.

The uncertainty about future strategy prevailing in Berlin introduced more than usual ambivalence into Ribbentrop's negotiation of the new Three Power Pact, as it came to be called, when signed in Berlin on 27 September 1940. Eight days earlier in Rome Ribbentrop had told Ciano that the Pact was to be directed against Russia and against the USA.[13] In Tokio, however, Stahmer and Ott offered the Japanese a secret protocol, pledging the Reich to work for improved Russo-Japanese relations and future co-operation with Russia within the framework of the Pact.[14] No sooner had they done so than they were instructed to withdraw the offer. It would, in fact, have been very acceptable to the Japanese Foreign Minister, Yosuka Matsuoka, who had come into office in

[12] *Wahn und Wirklichkeit:* E. Kordt (Stuttgart, 1948), pp.226-7
[13] *The Ciano Diaries:* ed. H. Gibson (New York, 1946), entry: 19.9.40
[14] *Germany and Japan,* op. cit., p.263

July 1940 as a convinced supporter of collaboration with Germany, but also wished to reach a definitive understanding with the Russians, in order to free Japan to take full advantage of the bright prospects opening up in South East Asia.

Two days before the Pact was signed Schulenburg informed Molotov, who complained that he ought to have been consulted, in accordance with the 1939 Treaty; *Pravda*'s comments on the Three-Power Pact were very reserved. This can hardly have surprised the signatories. It is true that Article 5 of the Pact affirmed that it 'in no way affects the political status existing at present between each of the three powers and Soviet Russia'; but this cannot have wholly erased the impression created in Russian minds by Article 3, by which the three powers undertook 'to assist one another with all political, economic and military means, if one of the three is attacked by a power at present not involved in the European War or in the Chinese-Japanese conflict'. This Article could, of course, be explained, with justice, as applying to the USA; but the fact remained that the Reich and Japan were now in a better position to bring pressure to bear upon the USSR, if need be. This impression was strengthened by the reference in Article 4 to the establishment of 'joint technical Commissions', a phrase replacing an original German preference for 'General Staff conversations'.[15]

The meat of the Pact, however, was contained in Articles 1 and 2, by which Japan 'recognizes and respects the leadership of Germany and Italy in the establishment of a new order in Europe', and Germany and Italy reciprocated as regards 'Greater East Asia'. But the USSR was a great power both in Europe and in Asia. What was to be her share of leadership in the two continents and what reason was there to suppose that her concept of a desirable 'new order' would have anything in common with that of the three signatory powers? Stalin had good cause to be in a mistrustful state of mind when in mid-

[15] *DGFP*, Series D, Vol. XI, pp.247-58

October he received from Ribbentrop a letter inviting him to send Molotov to Berlin to discuss possibilities of future co-operation and an improvement of Russo-Japanese relations, such as would enable the four powers concerned to act in concert for their common advantage.[16] Nevertheless Stalin replied promptly and favourably, being encouraged to do so, no doubt, by receiving from Matsuoka an offer to conclude a Japanese-Soviet pact of non-aggression. Matsuoka, who was at this stage acting in a reasonably straightforward way, asked Ribbentrop to use his good offices with Molotov during the latter's visit to Berlin.[17] That Hitler permitted this to be done is susceptible of various explanations. One is that he had not yet finally decided to attack Russia and was making a sincere attempt to bring about Soviet co-operation in the war against Britain, as well as Japanese co-operation in deterring the USA from intervening; this was indeed the impression he liked to give at a later date, when his great gamble had failed and Germany was engaged in a life and death struggle, which in the end he could not hope to win. An alternative explanation is that, whilst he certainly wanted Japan to play a deterrent role vis-a-vis the USA, he was so confident of defeating the USSR that he saw no need to engage the Japanese in this battle and was not prepared to pay any price for doing so.

Before examining these alternative explanations in the light of the conduct of negotiations with Molotov, it is convenient here to consider another motive Hitler must have had for wishing these to take place. We have stressed more than once that, however autocratic Hitler's behaviour had become, he still required the active collaboration of civil and military leaders and experts in bringing his plans to fruition, and to this end was accustomed to present these in terms calculated to appeal to minds unsympathetic with the unfettered ideological sweep of his own thought. Thus in mid-May 1942, after *Blitzkrieg* tactics against Russia had failed, he justified to his entourage the decision to attack on the ground that the unexpected Soviet strength proved that Stalin was about to invade and, if not forestalled, would have had Europe at his mercy. 'If he, Hitler, had listened to his badly informed Generals and waited, and the Russians, in accordance with these plans of theirs had stolen a march on us, there would have been hardly a chance of stopping their tanks on the well constructed road system of Central Europe.'[18] It was a specious claim, designed to convince his hearers that his decision, which had in fact ruined Germany, had been the salvation of Europe. Whether or not Hitler's own mind was already made up in the late autumn of 1940, he could not afford to ignore the hopes of those who believed that it was possible to come to an accommodation with Stalin. If the Fuehrer was to carry conviction with these men of little faith, it was clearly expedient to negotiate, or at least to go through the motions of doing so.

We have already seen that in late July the OKH was unhappy about the plan to invade Russia (see p.75). Even the submissive Keitel, though he would not brave the Fuehrer's wrath, expressed his concern to Ribbentrop at the end of August 1940. When Ribbentrop later approached Hitler, recommending that he make concessions to Stalin, extend the Three Power Pact and so 'neutralize the USA, isolate Britain and threaten her position in the Near East', Hitler was prepared to reveal rather more of his thinking to his sycophantic Foreign Minister than he had done in discussion with his Generals; he 'suspected Stalin of being under Jewish influence'. Once the war was over, Ribbentrop was able to set down, when it was too late, the only appropriate comment, namely that 'ideological grounds . . . always made the conduct of foreign policy impossible'.[19] The one persistent opponent of Barbarossa was Raeder, who was not informed of Hitler's intentions until the end of September 1940; the Admiral on that occasion argued in favour of diverting Stalin's

[18] *Tischgespraeche*, op. cit., p.150
[19] *Ribbentrop Memoirs*, op. cit., pp.147-50

ambitions in the direction of Iran and India.[20] Again in mid-November he pleaded with Hitler to postpone the invasion of Russia until after the defeat of Britain. The OKH, too, in anticipation of Molotov's visit, believed the Fuehrer shared their hope that it would be possible 'to integrate Russia into the front against England'.[21]

Hitler's diplomatic conversations at this period did indeed suggest that he was thinking in these terms. When he met Mussolini in Florence at the end of October 1940, he told him of Molotov's visit and the possibility of constituting 'a world front against England, stretching from Japan across Russia to Europe'. It must, however, be made clear to the Russians 'that it made little sense for them to look for expansion in regions where they would come up against the interests of Germany and Italy and only gain outlet to enclosed seas'. The context makes it plain that Hitler was not going to tolerate any Soviet expansion into the Baltic and Mediterranean, upon which the eyes of Communist Russians, no less than of Tsarist Russians, had long been focused. He also stressed to the *Duce* that he did not foresee the USSR becoming a fellow ally in the Three Power Pact; instead 'a special form of agreement between Russia and the partners of the Pact would be found'.[22]

This distinction was preserved in the draft agreement prepared by Ribbentrop, shown to Ciano and later handed to Molotov in Berlin. In it the Three Powers, as the one party, were to conclude with the USSR, as the other, an agreement 'to co-operate politically' in the course upon which the Three Powers were already embarked.[23] There was no clear definition of this course; yet Stalin, by committing himself to it, would be cutting himself off from the Anglo-Saxons, representing the only counterpoise to Fascist power. He was not to become a founder member of the Pact, but was being offered

[20] *Hitlers Strategie*, op. cit., p.190
[21] *Halder KTB*, Vol. II, p.158
[22] *Staatsmaenner*, op. cit., pp.158-65
[23] *DGFP*, Series D, Vol. XI, p.508

a junior partnership in an international crime syndicate, the objectives of which were to lie outside his control. Romania and Hungary, with whom Soviet relations were bad, had already signified their wish to adhere to the Pact; even the puppet state of Slovakia was visualized as a member. It is difficult to see how Hitler and Ribbentrop can seriously have supposed that Stalin would be willing to accept a status equivalent to that of these German satellites. In the event Hitler, in his first conversation with Molotov, did not actually propose Soviet adherence to the Pact; it was left to Molotov to bring up the subject. At the end of the conversation, which was brought to an untimely end by the air raid alarm, he assured Hitler that, 'in principle the participation of Russia in the Pact seemed to him entirely acceptable, on condition that Russia co-operated as a partner and was not merely the object of it'.[24]

In this first conversation Molotov had already brought up the question of Finland, which had conceded transit rights to German troops stationed in North Norway, as well as stressing Soviet interests in the Balkan and Black Sea areas. Soviet sources claim that, before the second conversation with Hitler on 13 November, Stalin sent instructions to Molotov to take a firmer line.[25] Hilger, the Russian-speaking Counsellor at the German Embassy in Moscow, who acted as interpreter, certainly noted a contrast between Molotov's demeanour on the first occasion and his 'stiffness and intransigence' at the second meeting.[26] This opened with an exchange of recriminations about fulfilment of the 1939 Treaty, leading to persistent questioning by Molotov about the reasons for increasing German links with Finland and Romania; he was unwilling to accept Hitler's assurances that these were solely connected with German economic needs. Turning next to Soviet concern with the Bosphorus, Molotov asked what the German attitude would be if the USSR offered

[24] *Staatsmaenner*, op. cit., p.176
[25] *Stalin and his Generals*: ed. S. Bialer (London, 1970), p.125
[26] *Incompatible Allies*, op. cit., pp.290-1

Bulgaria a territorial guarantee, similar to that granted by the Reich to Romania. Hitler, who had previously hinted at the possible need to take action against Greece to prevent British use of the airfield at Salonika, asked sharply whether the Bulgarians had requested a Soviet guarantee. There was no substantive discussion of prospective Russian interest in Iran and India, though Hitler made one of his grandiose allusions to a world coalition, including the USSR, which would represent 'a community of interests, stretching from North Africa to East Asia'.[27] Molotov concluded the conversation by thanking the Germans for the part they had played in improving Russo-Japanese relations.

It was, by any standards, an unsuccessful and inconclusive meeting; nobody had spoken so bluntly to the Fuehrer since Hindenburg dismissed him from his presence, without the seals of office, in August 1932. It seems likely that Molotov, who was more accustomed to plain speaking, did not realize how much Hitler had resented his intransigence, coming after a long autumn of abortive diplomatic interviews. However that may be, Molotov left Berlin believing that negotiations had only begun and that the next phase would be marked by another visit by Ribbentrop to Moscow. On return to Moscow Molotov composed a note, stating the maximum Soviet demands, which was given to Schulenburg on 25 November 1940. In the meantime Hitler had received the Hungarian Minister-President, Count Teleki, and Hungary's adherence to the Pact had been announced. Romanian adherence followed on 23 November 1940. The timing of these moves was insulting to the Russians, who had not yet made up their minds, and on 21 November 1940 a Tass communique was issued in Moscow, denying the statement in a German newspaper that the Soviet government had agreed to the adherence of Hungary.[28]

Contemporary Soviet writers find themselves in difficulty in recording the visit of Molotov to Berlin; one of

---

[27] *Staatsmaenner*, op. cit., p.188
[28] *Wahn und Wirklichkeit*, op. cit., p.287

them goes so far as to maintain that 'the repeated proposals of Hitler and Ribbentrop for "dividing up the world" encountered severe Soviet refusal even to speak of it'.[29] This is very far from the truth. The Soviet note of 25 November 1940 repeated Molotov's acceptance in principle of the adherence of the USSR to the Pact, though significantly referring to it as 'the Four Power Pact'; but the preconditions of adherence had been stiffened. Ribbentrop's draft agreement was to be supplemented by confidential protocols, specifying 'the focal points in the territorial aspirations' of the signatories; it was suggested that Russia's would lie 'south of the territory of the Soviet Union in the direction of the Indian Ocean'. Hitler's statement was taken at face value: Germany would require nothing more than a source of raw materials in Central Africa. The Soviet note proposed no fewer than five confidential protocols; one would have corresponded approximately to Ribbentrop's original proposal for Russia's 'focal point', though 'the Persian Gulf' was modestly substituted for 'the Indian Ocean'; two would have concerned respectively Turkey and a leased Soviet base in Bulgaria; the remaining two would have meant respectively Japanese renunciation of economic concessions in North Sakhalin and German withdrawal from Finland, in return for a guarantee of Hitler's economic requirements there.[30] In spite of several reminders, no reply was ever sent to this note.

It is, of course, clear that Hitler would not have acceded to such terms except under duress. It will become equally clear, as the narrative proceeds, that Stalin had no intention of confronting Hitler with such a stark alternative; indeed, as German silence persisted, the Russians showed themselves increasingly anxious to avert a recourse to arms. Subsequently, Hitler liked to tell his Generals, as for example Guderian,[31] that it was Molotov's visit that made him feel that war was inevitable; but this

[29] *Sonderakte Barbarossa:* L. Besymenski (Stuttgart, 1968), p.159
[30] *DGFP*, D, XI, p.714
[31] *Panzer Leader*, op. cit., p.141

conclusion would only have been justified if Stalin, failing to extract a reply to the Russian note, had begun to mobilize. Instead it was the Germans who were covertly mobilizing their forces in the East. The whole negotiation had been a 'blind'. The British were not threatening the supplies of nickel from Finland; they were not being allowed by their Greek allies to use the Salonika airfield from which the Romanian oil might have been threatened.[32] Hitler needed closer ties with Finland and Romania, not to defend himself against Britain, but to attack Russia. When Antonescu visited him on 22 November (i.e. before receipt of Molotov's note), there was discussion of 'the dark powers of Bolshevism and Judaism'; Hitler affirmed that the Reich and Romania must stand together against 'the Slav wave' and accused Britain of being prepared 'to sacrifice all Europe to Bolshevism'.[33] It is inconceivable that he would have used such language if he was still seriously contemplating collaboration with the USSR. Nor, if he had had in mind any real exchange of views with Molotov would he have insulted the latter's intelligence by the statement that the focal point of future German interests lay in Central Africa.

The conversations with Molotov, however, had served two useful ends. First, Hitler was now able to argue more convincingly that the only language the Russians could understand was force. Secondly, he had trapped them into showing their hand; indeed one recognized authority on Soviet-German relations concludes that if, as Hitler expected, the visit proved abortive, it 'would still serve German interests by providing Germany with real or fabricated statements of Russian demands which might be used to secure or keep in line reluctant allies in the coming struggle'.[34] The Turks and Bulgarians became more apprehensive about Soviet intentions, and the Finns and

[32] *Balkan Clue*, op. cit., p.92
[33] *Staatsmaenner*, op. cit., pp.206-8
[34] *Germany and the Soviet Union*: G. L. Weinberg (Leyden, 1954), p.140

Romanians more willing to co-operate with Hitler's aggressive designs. At the beginning of March 1941 Bulgaria adhered to the Three Power Pact, which was acquiring the open character of an anti-Bolshevist alliance. The Turks decided to batten down the hatches and ride out the storm as neutrals; they concluded a non-aggression pact with Bulgaria in mid-February, sat out the invasion of Greece and on the eve of Barbarossa signed a Treaty of Friendship with the Reich, which served to keep the Black Sea closed to intrusive warships.

One further pointer to Hitler's real attitude towards the negotiation with Molotov requires to be mentioned here. It will be recalled that at the end of July 1940 Marcks had been instructed to undertake preliminary planning for Barbarossa (p.75); after he had submitted an outline early in August, General Paulus, the new Quartermaster I, or Deputy Chief of Staff, was appointed on 6 September 1940 to draw up substantive plans.[35] We shall examine these in the next chapter; the point to be stressed here is that Paulus's first report was made to Halder on 29 October,[36] and by 13 November 1940, whilst Molotov was still in Berlin, Paulus completed the accompanying maps.[37] This documentation formed the main topic of the important discussion between Hitler and his Generals on 4 December 1940. Why did no preliminary discussion take place before Molotov's visit, in order to permit the war lord to judge, on the basis of the planning done since the great project of invasion was mooted nearly fourteen weeks earlier, what were the chances of speedy and lasting success?

During the intervening period there had been several developments affecting the Barbarossa undertaking. The most important of these was the operation against Greece, Marita, for which a detailed directive was issued on 13 December 1940; but there was also operation Felix against Gibraltar. On 27 November 1940 Halder and his

[35] *Halder KTB*, II, p.90
[36] Ibid., p.155
[37] Ibid., p.178

Chief of Operations, General Heusinger, discussed the impact of these operations upon Barbarossa and concluded that instead of pursuing the far-reaching objectives laid down originally by Hitler, it might be necessary to restrict operations to a line running from the Dnieper, through Smolensk, to the Baltic States. 'It is true that, starting from there, one could try an enveloping operation; but in the endless expanse of space this would have no prospect of success'.[38] These were grave considerations and it is strange that the Generals did not see fit to bring them to Hitler's attention as soon as he returned to Berlin from his diplomatic peregrinations; but the main responsibility rested with Hitler himself. A Generalissimo whose mind was still open to alternative possibilities would have wished to inform himself, before embarking on the critical interview with Molotov, what concessions he might need to make, or, if arms alone could decide, how good were his chances. It is impossible to escape the conclusion that Hitler already intended war and, without having examined the plans in detail, had convinced himself in advance that his war aims could readily be achieved. It was on 2 December 1940 that Halder recorded a remark of Hitler's Chief Adjutant, the egregious Schmundt, 'We shall be in Petersburg in three weeks' – to which Halder had the good sense to add two exclamation marks.[39] Schmundt must surely have been echoing his master's voice. This was no mere flight of fancy; it should be noted that the period of three weeks was also affirmed by Hitler in his conversation with Darlan on 12 May 1941.[40] This might be dismissed as an example of the Fuehrer's loud-mouthed style of diplomacy, but for the fact that members of his entourage took such statements as having been made *ex cathedra*; it then became treason to doubt them.

Molotov, during his visit, had discussed trading relations with Goering, who fended off complaints about delayed German deliveries.[41] A new economic agreement

[38] Ibid., p.198
[39] Ibid., p.203
[40] *Histoire de Vichy*, op. cit., p.431
[41] *Incompatible Allies*, op. cit., p.322

was signed on 10 January 1941 and the Russians showed good will by paying the equivalent in gold of RM 31.5 million for the Mariampol area of South West Lithuania, which had been occupied by the USSR, though assigned to the Reich by the secret additional protocol to the Treaty of 28 Septemeber 1939. The Russians had offered to pay the price in goods, including valuable raw materials, and were surprised by the German request for an immediate cash payment;[42] but they seem to have failed to draw the correct conclusion about the German wish not to prolong the terminal date for deliveries. In general, the economic exchanges, which continued until the last moment, served not only to fuel the German war machine, but also to convince Stalin that Hitler would not sacrifice so important a source of supply on the uncertain altar of war. He was not the first to be misled by ascribing to Hitler more rational processes of thought than, in fact, moved him.

The only positive outcome of the conversations in Berlin had been a step towards normalizing Soviet-Japanese relations. The secret of Hitler's early successes had lain, to a great extent, in his capacity to isolate his immediate opponent and concentrate the full force, or threat, of *Blitzkrieg* upon him. If this had still been his strategy, he would have egged on the Japanese to join him in attacking the USSR. Because his victories over France and the Netherlands had opened up such tempting prospects for Japan in South East Asia, it may be doubted whether an attempt to unleash the Japanese army against Russia would have succeeded; but the chances of success would have been very much better in the autumn of 1940 than at any subsequent date. The reason why Hitler adopted the opposite course of seeking to reconcile Japan and the USSR was not that he had become enamoured of Ribbentrop's 'continental bloc'; but that, in his overweening self-confidence, he was already looking beyond his coming victory over Russia to the next phase of his master-plan, when he

[42] *Wahn und Wirklichkeit,* op. cit., p.275

would have achieved hegemony in Europe and would be ready to take on the Anglo-Saxons. In this phase Japan had been assigned the important role of ensuring that, when the Americans finally intervened in the war, they would be tied down in the Pacific. As he said to his staff in mid-February 1941, Japan 'must put herself in possession of Singapore and of all the territory producing the raw materials she will need to continue the war, especially if the USA intervenes'.[43] This strategic aim was expressed in Directive 24 of 5 March 1941, which stipulated that nothing be said about Barbarossa to the Japanese.[44]

This secretiveness, which was typical of Hitler's relationship to his allies, took on almost the character of deception in the light of the reappointment of Oshima to Berlin in February 1941 and the visit in the following month of his Foreign Minister, Matsuoka, who was also Germanophile. Matsuoka travelled via Moscow, where he had an inconclusive meeting with Stalin. When he arrived in Berlin, it was soon clear to him that Russo-German relations had markedly deteriorated since November 1940, though Hitler assured him that he had no fear of a Soviet attack.[45] Ribbentrop claimed afterwards to have told Matsuoka that it would not be 'appropriate' for him to conclude a political agreement with the USSR during his return journey through Moscow.[46] He was therefore disagreeably surprised when Matsuoka did precisely that; the Soviet-Japanese agreement of 13 April 1941 provided that, in the event of either party becoming involved in war, the other would remain neutral. If the Germans had made their intentions clear and appealed to the Three Power Pact, even though its terms would not have covered, strictly speaking, the case of German aggression against Russia, it seems scarcely possible that Matsuoka could have acted in this way. It would certainly have been necessary for him to return to Tokio for

[43] *OKW/KTB*, I, p.328
[44] *Hitler's War Directives*, op. cit., pp.58-9
[45] *Staatsmaenner*, op. cit., p.244
[46] *DGFP*, D, XIII, p.84

consultations, which would have allowed time for further diplomatic intervention on the part of the Germans. Hitler, defending, as ever, his infallibility, claimed to have approved the course adopted by Matsuoka; this seems very improbable and there is, indeed, a sour note about the Fuehrer's later remark that Matsuoka had told him in Berlin that 'he could rely on Japan'.[47] Ribbentrop was franker and wrote after the war that the Japanese had acted 'behind our backs'.[48] This imputation, if not altogether true of Matsuoka, was certainly true of the Japanese Cabinet, which in his absence had decided to try to negotiate a settlement of outstanding differences with the USA. This policy, had it succeeded, would have completed the nullification of Hitler's aims in the Far East.

The obvious beneficiary was Stalin. Although Matsuoka, until his fall from office in mid-July 1941, claimed to have aided his German friends by leaving the Russians in uncertainty about Japanese intentions, Stalin knew from Sorge's reports that the decision to move south had been taken in Tokio; as early as July 1941 he was able to begin transferring troops from the Far Eastern to the European theatre.[49] Nevertheless Hitler derived one un-covenanted benefit from the Soviet-Japanese *rapproche-ment*, since it must have served to increase Stalin's false sense of security; the latter can hardly have ascribed to Hitler so contemptuous an attitude towards the Red Army that, in attacking it, he was willing to dispense with so manifest an asset as that of obliging it to keep up the strength of its Far Eastern Command. There was thus a double element of falsity about Stalin's notorious display of good feeling when at the Moscow railway station, after speeding Matsuoka's departure, he sought out Schulenberg and Krebs and enfolded each in turn in his simulated embrace.[50]

[47] *Tischgespraeche*, op. cit., p.109
[48] *Ribbentrop Memoirs*, op. cit., p.154
[49] *Soviet High Command*, op. cit., p.631
[50] *Halder KTB*, II, p.324

# VIII

## Barbarossa: Military Planning

Marcks, who drew up the first draft of an invasion plan, slightly improved on Kinzel's estimate of the number of Soviet infantry Divisions likely to be available to defend the western frontiers of the USSR (see p.74). He calculated that an equivalent number of attacking German Divisions would be deployed, but that within the respective totals the Germans would have a marked superiority in their 24 *Panzer* Divisions, since a substantial proportion of the Soviet mobile force was composed of cavalry (23 Divisions).[1] These calculations, which even at the outset did not envisage the numerical superiority that an attacking force would normally hope to enjoy, were predicated on two assumptions, neither of which was destined to be fulfilled. One was that Japanese pressure would oblige the Far Eastern strength of the Red Army to be maintained. We have seen, however, that Hitler made no effort to integrate Japan into his anti-Soviet plans; as late as mid-February 1941 he was insisting that the Japanese attack Singapore, not Vladivostok.[2] Marcks's second assumption was that the only forces to be deducted from Germany's maximum strength would be occupation troops remaining in 'Norway, Denmark and the West'.[3] In other words, no account was taken of operation Marita and the *Afrikakorps*, the need for which could not have been foreseen when Marcks reported early in August 1940.

On the other hand, Marcks credited the Red Army with a serious and rational plan of defence, which proved, when the time came, not to have existed. He expected that the Red Army, except on the Romanian front, where an attack on the oilfields might be launched, would fall back upon a line running southward from the River

---

[1] *German Strategy against Russia*, op. cit., App. IV
[2] *OKW/KTB*, I, p.328
[3] *German Strategy against Russia*, op. cit., App. I

Dvina to the Pripet Marshes and from there to the River Dniester, or even to the Dnieper, lying further east. Once the Red Army along this line had been broken, 'fighting in isolated battles they will soon succumb to the superiority of the German troops and leadership'.[4] This third assumption, namely the inferiority of the Russians in trained men, as well as in material, was better grounded; but understood in the ideological terms in which Hitler was accustomed to think, the deductions drawn from it became dangerously exaggerated and, as the odds against his success lengthened, these ideological deductions were made to justify every kind of imprudence. Thus at Hitler's conference on 5 December 1940, at which Paulus's revised plan was presented, the Fuehrer expressed himself as follows: 'In terms of weapons the Russian soldier is as inferior to us as the French. He has a few modern field batteries, everything else is old, reconditioned material . . . the bulk of the Russian *Panzer* force is poorly armoured. The Russian human material is inferior. The armies are leaderless . . .'[5] At this date the Germans did not know that the Russians had a heavy tank, the T34, superior to anything supplied to their *Panzer* Divisions; but they did know that, in order to bring these latter up to the required strength, they were themselves being obliged to recondition armoured vehicles seized from the French.

The over-confidence of the Fuehrer, who had so often before proved to be right, began to infect his Generals. On this point one can only agree with Professor Hillgruber: in so far as the Generals continued to object to Barbarossa, it was not so much because of the military risks involved, as because, for ending the war against Britain, the campaign seemed to them to be unnecessary.[6] This aspect of Barbarossa was still puzzling Halder as late as the end of January 1941; 'The purpose is not clear. We do not strike at the British and our economic

[4] Ibid.
[5] *Halder KTB*, II, p.214
[6] *Hitlers Strategie*, op. cit., p.211

potential will not be improved. The risk in the West should not be underestimated. It is even possible that Italy might collapse after losing her colonies and we find ourselves with a southern front through Spain, Italy and Greece. If we are then committed against Russia our position will become increasingly difficult'.[7]

As we saw in Chapter VI, Hitler largely ignored both the opportunities and the dangers of the Mediterranean theatre; but he did not underestimate the chances of trouble in Norway and Denmark, where in June 1941 he was holding back 8 Divisions, nor in France, where he had 38.[8] As he also had 8 Divisions in the Balkans and 2 in North Africa, Halder's estimate on the eve of Barbarossa was that he would actually have a smaller force than Marcks had envisaged; his 24 *Panzer* Divisions had dwindled to 19, and his 110 Infantry Divisions to 102.[9] Even this reduced force could only be put into the field by virtually eliminating the strategic reserve, which had been an important feature of Marcks's plan. As Halder was to write after the war, 'It is characteristic of Hitler's lack of strategic understanding that he never showed the slightest interest in the disposition and movement of the reserves . . .'[10]

The Luftwaffe's prospects were even less encouraging, since it was more actively engaged than the army against the RAF and targets in the West and Mediterranean. As Halder put it in mid-December 1940, 'For us it is a one-front war . . . for the Luftwaffe a two-front war . . .'[11] It has been estimated that some 1,150 combat aircraft were in the West, including Norway, and in the Mediterranean in June 1941;[12] this left about 2,770 combat aircraft available for the East, an unfavourable ratio of 4 or 5 to 1, according to one authority.[13] In mid-February, even

[7] *Halder KTB*, II, p.261
[8] *Hitlers Strategie*, op. cit., p.459
[9] *Halder KTB*, II, p.461
[10] *Hitler as War Lord*, op. cit., p.31
[11] *Halder KTB*, II, p.227
[12] *German Strategy against Russia*, op. cit., p.94n.
[13] *Soviet High Command*, op. cit., p.584

Hitler seems to have been momentarily discouraged on learning of the reported strength of the Red Air Force; he reacted typically by describing the coming conflict as unavoidable, rather than by reassessing his plans.[14]

What made these disparities so serious was that all the time estimates of Red Army strength were rising and Hitler's objectives were becoming more far-reaching. By the end of January 1941 the OKW was assuming that the Red Army would have on the European front 121 infantry Divisions, 25 cavalry Divisions and 31 mechanized Brigades.[15] In mid-March 1941, however, the OKH was still operating on rather more optimistic assumptions;[16] the problem was to know relative Soviet strength in the Far East and on the Turkish and Finnish borders, and Kinzel had to admit that little or no evidence was available.[17] At the beginning of April 1941 Kinzel conceded that 'Red Army strength in Europe must be taken to be greater than hitherto supposed', amounting to 171 infantry Divisions, 36 cavalry, and 40 mechanized Brigades; Halder sombrely recorded that the Finns and Japanese had always said as much.[18] At the final count before the invasion began these figures had for no stated reason been somewhat reduced.[19]

The plain fact is that the General Staff were almost entirely in the dark and had to rely heavily upon the expertise of their Military Attache in Moscow, General Koestring, and of Colonel Krebs, who replaced Koestring, when he fell ill in March 1941. Koestring had been in Moscow from 1931-33 and had taken up his post again in 1935; he was therefore familiar with the scene and his views were correspondingly influential. He had an important interview with Halder at the beginning of September 1940, at which he maintained that the Red Army was on the way up, but that it would take another

[14] *Halder KTB*, II, p.283
[15] *OKW/KTB*, I, p.290
[16] *Halder KTB*, II, p.316
[17] *Oberste Wehrmachtfuehrung*, op. cit., p.350
[18] *Halder KTB*, II, p.345
[19] Ibid., p.461

four years before it could regain the level achieved before Stalin's purges. He stressed the difficulties that would be encountered by mechanized units and qualified his remarks by a reference to the vigilance of the GPU (secret police or NKVD).[20] This report must have served to fortify Hitler's belief that it would be better to knock out Russia at once, rather than await a future date, when the Colossus might have come of age. A similar line of reasoning had disastrously influenced the thinking of an earlier German Chancellor some 26 years before.[21] (See p.18.)

Hans Krebs, who replaced Koestring in Moscow, was only 42; he was a young man on the make. Hilger records a talk with him in the spring of 1941; like all who knew Russia well, Hilger maintained that Russia could not be defeated. Krebs agreed, but added that Hitler would no longer listen to General Staff officers, 'after we warned him against the campaign against France . . .'[22] This was certainly a correct assessment of Hitler's attitude; Warlimont confirms that whatever advice contradicted the Fuehrer's preconceptions was written off as due to 'the defeatism of the General Staff'.[23] Such advice was not calculated to further the career of an ambitious young officer. This presumably explains the report given to Halder by Krebs early in May 1941, which was even more optimistic than Koestring's: 'Leadership markedly poor (depressing impression). Difference, as compared with 1933, is strikingly negative. Russia will need 20 years to regain the old level. Equipment with *matériel* is in progress. New fighter. New long-distance bomber. But the performance capacity of the pilots is meagre . . .'[24] Krebs was so expert at saying what Hitler wanted to hear that at the end of March 1945 he became the last Chief of the General Staff. His immediate predecessor, Guderian,

[20] Ibid., p.86
[21] *Deutschlands Rolle*, op. cit., pp.25, 44
[22] *Incompatible Allies*, op. cit., p.329
[23] *Im Hauptquartier*, op. cit., p.65
[24] *Halder KTB*, II, pp.396-7

was another who knew how to make his way. In August 1940 he had submitted to Hitler a report emphasizing the Red Army's weakness.[25] After the war, when Guderian was writing his reminiscences, he had forgotten about this report; he remembered only that the Russians had been underestimated and that Hitler had ignored Koestring's reports.[26]

In extenuation of the compliant attitude towards Hitler adopted by most of his staff officers, it might be argued that their low assessment of the Red Army was shared by Anglo-American Intelligence; in mid-June 1941 the Joint Intelligence Committee in London thought Russian resistance would last only six or seven weeks, and this view was endorsed by the Chief of the Imperial General Staff.[27] American military estimates were not much different. On the other hand, the wits of the German General Staff should have been sharpened by the prospect of hostilities against the USSR, which Britain and the USA were not contemplating. The Germans had two additional advantages. First, they had a standard of comparison, since seven years earlier they had known the Red Army well. In the second place, the Germans were able, if they had wished, to profit from the experiences of their Japanese allies, who had been disagreeably impressed by the fighting of Red Army units under Zhukov during the last eleven days of August 1939. At Khalkin-Gol Soviet armour and artillery had 'proved far superior to the Japanese';[28] Zhukov had used tanks and motorized infantry to make deep penetrations into the enemy lines, showing that Soviet tacticians were beginning to master the principles of modern warfare even before the Germans taught them how to do it. Moreover the giant T34 tank had made its first appearance, though in small numbers.

However rigidly Soviet society was policed, the

25 *Hitlers Strategie*, op. cit., p.225
26 *Panzer Leader*, op. cit., p.151
27 *Grand Strategy*: ed. J. R. M. Butler (London, 1957), Vol. II, p.543
28 *Soviet High Command*, op. cit., pp.536-7

Germans could have learned simply from budgetry estimates that the Russians were investing massively in
defence, which in 1941 amounted to no less than 43% of
total state spending.[29] Between 1939 and 1941 125 new
Divisions were added to the Red Army and in 1941
annual production of the T34 reached 1,100.[30] The
Germans could not, of course, have known these exact
figures, but it is indeed astonishing that at the beginning
of 1941 they were still crediting the Russians with fewer
infantry Divisions on their Western front than had been
notified to the Anglo-French during the abortive negotiations in Moscow in the summer of 1939.[31] It is difficult to believe that these latter figures can have remained
secret very long. When after the war Zhukov was shown
Paulus's estimate of Red Army strength in December
1940, he commented, 'It is inconceivable that the Germans
could have assumed that they were facing at the front a
foe with a strength of less than three million men.'[32] In
fact Soviet historians, though anxious to admit nothing
that might detract from the Red Army's laurels, concede
that in June 1941 the USSR had nearly five million men
under arms.[33] A very high proportion must by June 1941
have been on the European front, and one British authority gives them a superiority of 30 Divisions over the
Germans and Finns combined.[34] Why they made such a
poor use of this superiority is a matter we shall consider
in the final chapter.

The persistent tendency to underestimate the size of
the opposing force must in large measure be ascribed to
wishful thinking; it was matched by the rooted belief that
the enemy's fighting power was negligible. This belief
is partly explicable in terms of the traditional German
assumption of superiority over the Slav, which had been
fortified both by Nazi ideology and by the collapse of

[29] *Stalin and his Generals*, op. cit., p.59
[30] Ibid., p.157
[31] *Soviet High Command*, op. cit., p.527
[32] *Sonderakte Barbarossa*, op. cit., p.248
[33] Ibid., p.249
[34] *Soviet High Command*, op. cit., p.584

Russian resistance in the First World War. There was, however, another factor which strongly coloured German thinking after 1937, namely Stalin's purge of the Red Army's officer corps. Marshal Tukhachevsky, who was arrested in mid-May, partly on evidence supplied by Heydrich and his SD, was not only the ablest of the Russian military leaders, but was the best known in Western Europe. Stalin's notorious xenophobia meant that a high proportion of liquidated officers had connections with the Reichswehr in happier days. John Erickson estimates that between 20,000 and 25,000 officers were removed: 'By the end of 1938 only some 39% of the officers at a level running from divisional commander to Marshal remained as compared with the position in May 1937.'[35] The most telling evidence against Tukhachevsky was derived from a White Russian emigré, General Skoblin, who may well have been a double agent. Before submitting this evidence to Hitler, Heydrich supplemented it with forged and pilfered material designed to incriminate the German General Staff, which was a special object of his hatred.[36] This latter objective was no doubt uppermost in his mind at that date, and the later claim that it had all along been the intention of the SD to ruin the Red Army was most likely devised with the benefit of hindsight.

However that may be, Stalin, who paid the SD the asking price (3 million gold roubles) for their evidence, certainly used it to bring about a paralysis in Soviet military leadership, which greatly impressed contemporary observers. Subsequent events seemed to confirm the experts' diagnosis. The bearing of Soviet troops encountered by German officers in September 1939 on the demarcation line in Poland struck the latter unfavourably, and deficiencies in equipment were brought to the Fuehrer's attention.[37] The winter war of 1939-40 against Finland provided fresh confirmation, and the German

[35] Ibid., p.506
[36] *The Labyrinth:* W. Schellenberg (New York, 1956), pp.25-8
[37] *Inside the Third Reich*, op. cit., p.169

General Staff noted that, 'The Russian mass is no match for an Army with modern equipment and superior leadership.'[38] No attempt seems to have been made to correlate this evidence with that provided by Soviet success against the Japanese; the latter information, because it did not fit preconceptions, was simply rejected. That there were serious discontents and deficiencies in the Red Army cannot be denied; but, as we shall see in Chapter X, Hitler deliberately adopted a form of warfare that precluded exploitation of these weaknesses and obliged the great majority of Russians to rally round Stalin.

Having now considered the size of the forces confronting one another, we must turn to the plan of campaign. The inadequacy of the German forces available was aggravated by two features of the land mass before them. First, it expanded as they advanced, straining the links between Army Groups and stretching them all the way from Leningrad to the Caucasus. Secondly, the vast front was dissected by the Pripet Marshes, creating a gap of nearly 200 miles, in which armour could operate only with difficulty. Marcks had set himself the limited objective of so crippling the Russian armed forces as 'to make Russia incapable of entering the war as an opponent of Germany in the foreseeable future'. He expected that the campaign could be successfully concluded on a line running from Archangel to the Upper Volga (Gorki) to the Don River (Rostov).[39] His successor, Paulus, persisted in this belief, in spite of certain ominous remarks made by Hitler at his conference with his Generals on 31 July 1940. Hitler then spoke of 'the destruction of Russia's vital power' and added that gaining a certain expanse of territory would not be enough; the oil-producing area of Baku on the Caspian was also designated as 'part of a later operation'.[40] Halder and Paulus went ahead without examining the implications of these remarks, though after the war the latter described the task facing the planners

[38] *Soviet High Command*, op. cit., p.548
[39] *German Strategy against Russia*, op. cit., App. I
[40] *Halder KTB*, II, p.50

as 'far beyond German strength'.[41] In retrospect, Halder also gives the impression that he thought Hitler's objectives were limited: 'Occupation of sizeable parts of the Ukraine, of White Russia and of the Baltic States would have provided a bargaining counter for peace negotiations'.[42]

The Fuehrer conference of 5 December 1940, at which Paulus's plan was presented, did little to clarify the exact nature of the objectives. Halder was left with the impression that 'the furthest objective' was to reach a point from which Russian air attacks on the Reich would no longer be possible. This implied the continued existence of a Russian state in some form. On the other hand, Hitler repeated in even more emphatic terms his earlier remarks about the need 'to destroy Russian living forces; nothing should be left capable of bringing about regeneration . . .'[43] Presumably his hearers dismissed this as the Fuehrer's rhetoric – never a prudent attitude to adopt with Hitler. There also arose a new source of ambiguity, which was to have serious consequences. Marcks had come to the conclusion that the main weight of the offensive ought to fall north of the Pripet Marshes and that, within this northern sector, Moscow should be regarded as the major objective.[44] A variant had, however, been drafted in the OKW by Colonel Lossberg; whilst it bears an earlier date, it was not submitted to Jodl until mid-November 1940, according to the recollection of Warlimont, who was Lossberg's immediate superior.[45] There is no definite evidence that Hitler ever saw it, but his thinking could, of course, have been influenced through Jodl.

Lossberg agreed with Marcks that the main thrust, which in Paulus's more elaborate version had become Army Group Centre, should fall north of Pripet; but the variant envisaged that, after a 'break through in the gen-

[41] *IMT*, Vol. VII, p.259
[42] *Hitler as War Lord*, op. cit., p.40
[43] *Halder KTB*, II, p.210
[44] *German Strategy against Russia*, op. cit., App. I
[45] *Im Hauptquartier*, op. cit., p.151

eral direction of Moscow', strong forces should turn north 'in order to cut off the Russians facing the north wing' (i.e. the Army Group advancing towards Leningrad).[46] This tactic was calculated to appeal to Hitler, who kept stressing the need to encircle and destroy Russian forces, rather than simply driving them back into the interior of the country. At the December conference he used the words: 'Moscow not very important.'[47] Twelve days later he instructed Jodl to insert in the draft Directive (which at the same time received the designation Barbarossa) an amendment whereby Army Group Centre would 'swing strong units of its mobile forces to the north, in order to destroy the enemy forces fighting in the Baltic area, acting in conjunction with Army Group North . . . in the general direction of Leningrad'. Only after the capture of Leningrad and Kronstadt was the advance on Moscow to be resumed.[48] On the following day the amended Directive was signed by Hitler as No. 21.

Hitler reiterated at a conference at the Berghof on 9 January 1941 his emphasis on 'the swift envelopment of the Baltic area'; he added that 'the Baku area must be occupied'.[49] This stress on the two extremities of the vast front should, to say the least, have provoked some discussion, which Brauchitsch might have linked to a remark he had made earlier, namely that the forces assigned to Marita would not be available for Barbarossa. He could also have brought into the open the point that expanding tasks were being given to a diminishing force and, in the process, the wings were being strengthened at the expense of concentration at the centre (Moscow). Instead of saying any of these things, the Generals appear to have listened in respectful silence, whilst Hitler reached his peroration with the observation that, 'When this operation is carried out, Europe will hold its breath.' A certain breathlessness on the part of the Generals would also

---

[46] *German Strategy against Russia*, op. cit., App. II
[47] *Halder KTB*, II, p.211
[48] *OKW/KTB*, I, p.233
[49] Ibid., p.258

have been in order. It seems clear from later developments in the summer of 1941 that they were only paying lip-service to Hitler's down-grading of Moscow as main objective, in the expectation that they would be able to circumvent it when operations actually began. If this was indeed their attitude, events showed how dangerous it was to embark upon so massive an undertaking without an agreed understanding of the phases of its execution. Army Group Centre, as one authority has it, 'remained virtually passive within 200 miles of Moscow from the beginning of August to the first week in October'.[50]

Commanding officers of the older generation, brought up to regard war not as a form of genocide, but as a means of achieving a political aim, were asking themselves how the war against Russia was to be brought to an end. This question must have been linked in their minds with differences of opinion about the importance of Moscow, even though Napoleon's experience warned against the assumption that seizure of the capital city would be decisive. Rundstedt's biographer claims it was the Field-Marshal's view that 'war with Russia might last for years'.[51] There is no evidence that he expressed this view to Hitler; but Field-Marshal Bock, who was received by Hitler on 2 February 1941, did put the crucial query how the Russians could be forced to make peace; the reply that, if necessary, German mobile forces would push on to Ekaterinburg cannot have been reassuring.[52] It was not only Field-Marshals who had their doubts; two of Bock's staff officers, who knew Russia well, attended a briefing on the eve of the invasion by his Chief of Staff, General v. Greiffenburg, who prophesied that they would be in Moscow in five or six weeks. When they enquired whether that would end the war, he replied with tolerant good humour, 'We won't cudgel our brains about that.'[53] The tendency to leave it to the Fuehrer's intuition

[50] *The Russo-German War:* A. Seaton (London, 1971), p.152
[51] *Rundstedt the Soldier,* op. cit., p.104
[52] *German Strategy against Russia,* op. cit., p.142
[53] *Gegen Hitler u. Stalin:* W. Strik-Strikfeldt (Mainz, 1970), p.15

had thus infected even Greiffenburg, who had been serving in the OKH under Halder until October 1940.

Over-optimism and faulty intelligence were together responsible for the fatal belief that the Russians would have to stand and fight west of the Dnieper and, after being defeated there, would collapse because of the loss of so much of their industrial potential. The error was compounded by lack of a long-range bomber force to attack Soviet production centres. After the war Koestring claimed to have warned of great industrial areas beyond the Ural mountains; but, if he did so, his warnings left as little trace on the minds of the planners as in their records. Halder and the Chief of his Operations Branch debated this question in mid-December 1940 and concluded that 32% of Soviet war production was in the Ukraine and 44% in the Moscow and Leningrad areas, leaving only the balance of 24% further east.[54] Like so much of their statistical information, this proved no better than guess-work. Canaris, the Chief of Military Intelligence, though personally opposed to the invasion, fed into the machine the reassuring and misleading information that the main industrial centres in the USSR and the main areas producing raw materials were linked only by single-track railways.[55] It was as if the Germans were incapable of believing that the USSR was fast becoming a modern industrial power.

The most singular feature of the whole planning operation, however, was the way in which, as the complexity of the campaign and the disparity of forces became more apparent, the allotted time schedule grew shorter. The first estimate, made at Hitler's conference at the end of July 1940 when his objectives still seemed to be of a relatively limited character, had been five months.[56] Making the assumption – and it was a large one – that *Blitzkrieg* methods so successfully applied in Poland and France were equally applicable in the much vaster and

[54] *Halder KTB*, II, p.236
[55] *Labyrinth*, op. cit., p.191
[56] *Halder KTB*, II, p.49

rougher terrain of the USSR, this was not an unreasonable estimate to make at a time when it was thought the Wehrmacht would have at least numerical equality. The campaign, begun in May, would have ended before weather conditions deteriorated, preventing the technical superiority of German arms from having its full impact. Marcks postulated a maximum duration of 17 weeks, though it will be recalled that he was restricting himself to a line from the Upper Volga to the Don.[57] Paulus, whilst further dispersing his forces, reduced the period to 10 weeks.[58] By the time his plan was presented to Hitler at the beginning of December, the starting date had slipped to the end of May.[59]

It would have been prudent, at that stage, to re-examine all the assumptions on which the High Command was basing its hopes of knocking out the USSR in one campaign. This would necessarily have included an analysis of the economic base available to the Germans for sustaining a two-front war for a minimum period of 18 months without access to Russian raw materials. As we shall see in the next chapter, this was the very point on which Thomas, the responsible staff officer, had most serious misgivings. The High Command, instead of insisting on presenting these doubts to Hitler, took refuge in increasingly unrealistic time schedules, in order to convince themselves that victory would still be achieved by the autumn of 1941. In the end it was as if collective madness had seized them; it was not only Hitler, who raved about victory in three weeks (see p.112); even Brauchitsch at the end of April 1941 summed up the prospects as follows: 'Massive frontier battles to be expected; duration up to four weeks. But in further development only minor resistance is then still to be reckoned with.'[60] There is no gainsaying the verdict of Zhukov: 'The German forces invaded the Soviet Union intoxicated

[57] *Hitlers Strategie*, op. cit., p.229
[58] Ibid., p.367
[59] *Halder KTB*, II, p.210
[60] *IMT*, XXVI, 873-PS

by their easy victories over the armies of Western Europe
. . . and firmly convinced both of the possibility of an easy
victory over the Red Army and of their own superiority
over all other nations . . .'[61]

It remains to consider the relevance to the military
planning of the Greek and Yugoslav campaigns, and the
degree of importance attached by Hitler to co-operation
with minor allies. At Hitler's conference on 9 January
1941 he characterized German relationships with three
key Balkan countries; Romania was friendly; Yugoslavia
cool; Bulgaria loyal, but hesitating to join the Three
Power Pact for fear of Russia.[62] King Boris was, in fact,
waiting till German strength had built up in Romania;
he finally adhered on 1 March 1941 and on the following
day German troops began entering his country. In anticipation of this development, the Soviet Ambassador had
already lodged a protest in Berlin. As these German troop
movements could only mean pressure on Greece, British
troops began landing on the Greek mainland a few days
later. It is interesting to speculate whether, if the British
forces had confined themselves to the occupation of
Crete, Hitler would have limited himself to driving the
Greeks out of Macedonia and occupying Salonika and the
north coast of the Aegean, which was all that had been
envisaged in the first Marita Directive of 13 December
1940.[63] This would have been enough to prevent the
Greeks from pursuing their offensive against the Italians,
and to secure the rear of Army Group South, when it
began to move against Russia. It was not until 17 March
1941 that Hitler finally decided to occupy the whole
mainland of Greece.[64]

It was on the same day that Prince Paul, Regent of
Yugoslavia, gave way with great misgiving to Hitler's
pressure upon him to join the Three Power Pact; but he
stipulated that German troops and supplies for the in-

[61] *Marshal Zhukov's Greatest Battles:* H. E. Salisbury (London,
1969), p.154
[62] *OKW/KTB*, I, p.256
[63] Ibid., p.224
[64] Ibid., p.360

vasion of Greece should not pass through his country. This restriction was particularly irksome to the Germans in mounting the extended operation, since no railway entered Greece from Bulgaria and the Germans, deprived of the Yugoslav railway system, would be forced to move troops and heavy equipment along deplorable Bulgarian roads at an unfavourable time of year. Moreover the Greek-Yugoslav frontier, unlike the Greek-Bulgarian frontier, was unfortified.[65] Paul's formal adherence to the Pact took place on 25 March 1941, one week before the invasion of Greece was due to begin. His misgivings proved justified, however, and on the 27 March he was removed by a popular uprising, together with his Germanophile government. Although the new government of General Simovic, serving under the young King Peter, did not denounce the Three Power Pact, Hitler had by one o'clock the same day decided to destroy Yugoslavia; he had had enough of diplomatic negotiation with recalcitrant Slavs; moreover the Yugoslav railways would be invaluable in bringing troops back from Greece in time to take part in Barbarossa.

After the initial attempt to crush the USSR in one swift campaign had failed, Hitler liked to maintain that his lightning strike against Yugoslavia had finally destroyed Stalin's hopes of creating in the Balkans 'a favourable spring-board to attack us and so attack all Europe'.[66] It was presumably Jodl's acceptance of this interpretation of Hitler's actions that led the General after the war to write of Barbarossa that the Fuehrer made 'the final decision only on 1 April 1941; for at this time an event occurred that effectively delayed the beginning of the attack against the almost completely assembled Soviet forces by four or five weeks. For Hitler it was like a beacon that revealed Stalin's intentions. It was the military coup in Belgrade.'[67] It would be difficult to compress more misinformation within the scope of three sentences.

[65] *Balkan Clue*, op. cit., p.65
[66] *Tischgespraeche*, op. cit., pp.260-1
[67] *Hitler: Man and Military Leader*, op. cit., App. II

Jodl chose an arbitrary date, for which no supporting evidence exists, and tried to bolster it by implying that Hitler only narrowly forestalled a Soviet invasion. We shall consider this legend of a preventive war in the last chapter; meanwhile it is only necessary to point out that Hitler had been complaining of Stalin's intentions since the summer of 1940. It is moreover clear that the rising in Belgrade was a popular movement against German pressure and owed nothing directly to Soviet support, though some British influence was undoubtedly exerted.

Stalin seems to have overestimated the possibilities of Yugoslav resistance and imprudently concluded a treaty with the new government on the very day (6 April 1941) that the Germans launched their assaults on Yugoslavia and Greece. When on the same day Schulenburg called on Molotov to inform him of the German invasion of Yugoslavia, Molotov made no mention of the treaty.[68] One month later he made a conciliatory, if pusillanimous, gesture by breaking off diplomatic relations with the Yugoslav government in exile. Stalin may have played his cards badly, but the decision to spread the war to the Balkans was not his. Nor did the two major partisan movements, which soon developed in Yugoslavia, owe their birth to Soviet inspiration, a significant factor in the post-war history of Europe. They profited, however, by the precipitate withdrawal of German troops required for Barbarossa which meant that only four Divisions of security forces remained behind.[69]

Partisan activity was the main Yugoslav contribution to Germany's ultimate defeat; the careful researches of Martin van Creveld have disproved the earlier assumption that the coup in Belgrade bore the major responsibility for delaying the start of Barbarossa, with the result that winter overtook the Germans on the inhospitable steppes of Russia. This was another of Hitler's alibis. We have already seen that by the spring of 1941 the High Command was almost unanimous in believing that the

[68] *Soviet High Command*, op. cit., p.573
[69] *Balkan Clue*, op. cit., p.165

Red Army would suffer defeat long before the winter, even though a few older sceptics doubted that it would bring peace. It is in any case an error to suppose that 15 May 1941, the date mentioned in the Barbarossa Directive, was a firm date for the start of military operations; it was, in fact, the date by which the preparations were to be concluded, so that Hitler would be free at any time thereafter to give the word.[70] At the beginning of February Halder had drawn Hitler's attention to the conflicting demands of Marita and Barbarossa,[71] and when Marita in its extended form was decided upon, Halder assumed at once (28 March 1941) that inclusion of Yugoslavia in the campaign would mean both further delay and more time for preparation: 'We should make the best use of the postponement, which gives us four weeks'.[72] This was a reasonable estimate, in view of his original assessment that Marita, even in its limited form, would take 'at least three to four weeks'.[73] The principal causes of delay, apart from weather conditions, were Hitler's decision to occupy the whole of Greece, the High Command's overestimate of the forces required, and, above all, overconfidence in a facile victory over the Red Army.

It is a striking fact that the Germans, who wrote off the Red Army so contemptuously, should have overestimated both the time required for the Greek-Yugoslav campaign and the forces needed. Even Hitler approached the lesser campaign more cautiously, if one can credit Goebbels' comment at his confidential press briefing on the day Marita began that, 'the Fuehrer estimates the duration of the operation at about two months'.[74] In the event German armour got to Salonika by 9 April; Belgrade fell four days later; Yugoslavia capitulated on 17 April and Greece on 23 April, though Crete, which had earlier been excluded from Marita, was not completely in German hands until 1 June 1941. Of the troops

[70] *Hitler's War Directives*, op. cit., p.49
[71] *OKW/KTB*, I, p.360
[72] *Halder KTB*, II, p.333
[73] *Oberste Kriegsfuehrung*, op. cit., p.325
[74] *Totaler Krieg*, op. cit., p.179

assigned to the campaign four Divisions and one SS
Regiment never saw action.[75] There were two favourable
by-products: the campaign provided camouflage for the
Barbarossa build up, and the Yugoslav railways expedited
the return of units needed against Russia.

This does not mean that Marita was without influence
on Barbarossa. Marshal List, whose 12th Army was to
have formed the spearhead of Army Group South in the
Ukraine, was given the new post of Commander-in-Chief
South-East. As Hitler had also detached General Kleist's
*Panzer* Group to operate north of the Carpathians,
Rundstedt's Army Group South, which included a motley
array of Romanian, Italian, Hungarian, Croatian and
Slovakian contingents, was too much weakened to be able
to attempt a major pincer movement against the Red
Army, and this was only accomplished in August by with-
drawing forces from Army Group Centre. The great
battle of Kiev was then won, but the advance on Moscow
was delayed. Moreover Hitler's decision, taken as late as
25 April 1941, to seize Crete led to casualties heavier
than in the whole of the rest of the Balkan campaign,
falling with particular weight on General Student's parachute Division.[76]

One significant result of the swift and decisive victory
was to increase still further Hitler's overweening self-
confidence; as he said on 31 May 1941, 'To the German
soldier nothing is impossible!'[77] This was undoubtedly
the chief reason why no effort was made, in the light of
the early completion of Marita, to bring forward the date
for Barbarossa. On the last day of April 1941 Hitler
settled upon 22 June, after rejecting the OKH proposal
of 25 June.[78] The OKH were in no hurry, partly because
of unfavourable weather, resulting in swollen rivers, and
partly because of deficiencies of *matériel*. As it was, the
new campaign began with most of the vehicles for the

[75] *Balkan Clue*, op. cit., p.166
[76] Ibid., p.170
[77] Ibid., p.177
[78] IMT, XXVI, 873-PS: *Oberste Kriegsfuehrung*, op. cit., p.383

new *Panzer* Divisions coming from French stock, which Guderian regarded as unsuited to conditions in the East.[79]

Hitler's self-confidence also led him to disregard the possibility of involving his major allies in Barbarossa; Italy and Japan were only informed officially a few hours before the invasion began, though Hitler appears to have told Oshima on 3 June of the coming attack, without mentioning the date.[80] Mussolini, at his own wish, sent an Army Corps to join in the anti-communist crusade; the Japanese were not even asked, until after the invasion had started, to prevent supplies reaching the Russians via Vladivostok.

At the beginning of February Hitler had told Halder that the minor allies, with the exception of Romania, were only to be informed of Barbarossa at the last moment.[81] It was necessary to assign an active role to Romania; in any case Antonescu's verbal excursions into the ideological world of anti-Semitism and anti-Slavism had earned him the Fuehrer's confidence. As late as 18 March 1941 Hitler was insisting that the co-operation of Hungary and Slovakia was only needed for logistical reasons;[82] Hungary and Romania were uneasy bedfellows in any alliance. Halder and Rundstedt, however, were concerned about the concentration of Soviet forces confronting Army Group South and succeeded in circumventing Hitler's wishes; Hungary declared war five days after Barbarossa had begun. Hitler had assigned to Finland the task of containing the Red Army in the Leningrad area, with the possibilities of a more northerly drive to Murmansk. Marshal Mannerheim was keen to rectify Finland's frontiers, but not to embark on rash adventures; it was not until after the Red Air Force had raided Helsinki that on 25 June 1941 he declared war. Bulgaria remained in diplomatic relations with the USSR, leaving Slovakia as the only Slav country to take an active part in the anti-

[79] *Panzer Leader*, op. cit., p.143
[80] *Japan u. der Fall Barbarossa*: A. Hillgruber in *Wehrwissenschaftliche Rundschau*, 1968.
[81] *OKW/KTB*, I, p.299
[82] Ibid., p.361

Slav crusade. The great German army, at the height of its power, marched out to war for the last time, accompanied by little more than armed camp followers; it was marching into the unknown under the direction of a man with a megalomanic belief in his destiny. But even megalomaniacs have moments of insight after the event and in one of these Hitler spoke the truth: 'On the 22nd of June, a door opened before us, and we didn't know what was behind it . . . the heavy uncertainty took me by the throat.'[88]

[83] *Hitler's Table Talk*, op. cit., p.71

## IX

## Barbarossa: Economic Planning

Divergencies between Hitler and his Generals, relating to outlook and background, have been sufficiently stressed in these pages; but there was one traumatic experience they had in common – Germany's defeat and humiliation in the First World War. From this terrible lesson Hitler and his Generals had begun by drawing certain conclusions in common. One of these was that Germany should not again become involved in a two-front war, and Hitler had formulated this in his early speeches and in *Mein Kampf* as meaning that Germany must choose between friendship with Britain and friendship with Russia. On this issue, as we have seen, his views and those of his Generals for many years parted company; but it was clear to all, broadly speaking, that the Reich, in order to fight a major war, must either be free of the British blockade, which had wrought such havoc in 1917-18, or must have access to Russian raw materials and transit trade. There were two other shared conclusions, based on First World War experience: one was that steps must be taken to prevent a collapse on the home front; the other that mobile warfare, characterized by lightning strokes, must safeguard the Reich against again becoming involved in a war of attrition, which she could not win.

These linked concepts found their expression in the term *Blitzkrieg* which comprehended not only use of tanks and dive-bombers at the front, but also use of longer-range bombers against civilian targets to paralyse the will to resist. Seen from the 'receiving end', *Blitzkrieg* looked very much like 'total war'; but from the German end it was, in fact, a means of avoiding total war and allowing the German civilian to reap the benefits of a succession of quick victories, without enduring the privations inseparable from a war of attrition. It was not until after Stalingrad that Hitler finally admitted that this policy had failed; as one authority has written, 'Total war was Hitler's nemesis, not his design.'[1] By 1943 the Reich was also on the receiving end of incomparably more severe punishment than had been meted out earlier to Warsaw, Rotterdam, Coventry and Belgrade.

Hitler and those of his Generals who thought about such matters disagreed about the need to impose the disciplines of total war on the civilian population at the beginning of the war. This was partly because they also disagreed about the political implications of *Blitzkrieg*, which Hitler regarded as a means of rapidly eliminating opponents in series, before they could effectively combine against him. The more cautious attitude of the Generals was linked to their scepticism whether the Fuehrer would, in practice, succeed in arriving at his ambitious goals without precipitating a major war, likely to escalate into a world war. Few of them at first believed that the statesmen of the world would be so lacking in vision and determination as to allow Hitler to isolate and successively eliminate Austria, Czechoslovakia and Poland, though by 1940 they had enough confidence in Hitler's pact with Stalin to accept that the latter would sit back and watch the elimination of France. The fact that potential and actual opponents facilitated Hitler's conquests in this way was one of the principal reasons for his domination over the minds of his previously sceptical staff officers, and for the lack of concerted and positive action on the military side of the resistance movement.

None the less not all the Generals were prepared to abandon their original insistence that Germany should not incur the risks of major war, which might develop, as in 1914-18, into a war of attrition, until two conditions were satisfied. One was that time be allowed to expand the miniature Reichswehr of 1933 by degrees into a well trained force with an *esprit de corps* that would be insurance against the disintegration that had occurred at the end of the First World War. The second stipulation was that Germany should rearm in depth with massive

[1] *Design for Total War*, op. cit., p.93

stocks of strategic raw materials and reserves of production plant and manpower adequate to ensure that she could survive a long war, if it came. These hopes were not to be realized, because they conflicted with the furious tempo of rearmament imposed by Hitler for reasons of ideology and personal ambition, which we have already discussed. Before Hitler came to power, Schleicher had planned to expand the Reichswehr from 7 to 21 Divisions by 1938; but in practice by 1939 Germany had already 103 Divisions, including 50 reserve Divisions.[2]

This was an impressive achievement in military terms, but the cost in terms of economic stability had been high, especially as it had been accompanied not by austerity for the population as a whole, but by a general improvement in the living standards of the workers under conditions of full employment and controlled prices. Heavy imports, both of foodstuffs and of strategic raw materials, together with channelling so large a proportion of productive resources into unproductive armaments, had by 1936 almost exhausted foreign exchange reserves. There was also a manpower shortage, which was aggravated by an ideological reluctance on the part of the Nazis to see women going into factories, instead of confining themselves to children, church and kitchen (*Kinder, Kirche, Kueche*). It was an economic problem that Hitler never solved, except by conquests, which replenished depleted foreign exchange and raw materials, as war booty, and press-ganged labour from defeated countries. In 1936, however, Hitler was not yet ready to embark on the Tamerlane phase of his strange career. He therefore adopted his usual expedient in a crisis, namely that of appointing an overlord with plenary powers – in this instance Goering.

The basic aim of Goering's Four-Year Plan was to maintain the tempo of rearmament, without a perceptible lowering of living standards, until such time as Germany was ready for war. The alternative policy was that advocated by Schacht and Goerdler, nationalists of an older

[2] *Arms, Autarky and Aggression,* op. cit., p.120

generation, who did not regard plunder as a legitimate motive for war, though in the right circumstances the rectification of frontiers might be. They held that in a few years Germany could become strong enough to remedy her main grievances, with or without war, if she moderated the rate of rearmament and developed profitable trading relations with the outside world. This alternative was completely alien to Hitler's way of thinking, and in August 1936 he expressed himself in a memorandum, which he gave to Goering. Germany, Hitler declared, with such help as she could get from Italy and Japan, was the only barrier against the assault of Bolshevism on Europe. Therefore, 'it is impossible to exaggerate the extent to which, and the speed at which, our military potential must be effectively deployed. . . . Therefore to this task all other desiderata must be unconditionally subordinated. . . . In four years the German economy must be capable of supporting a war.'[3]

The main expedient adopted by Goering to meet Hitler's demands was autarky; by developing '*ersatz*' products, such as synthetic rubber (buna), the Reich would save foreign exchange by reducing imports. On this tide the ingenious directors of *I.G. Farben* rode to power and notoriety. Autarky also meant developing indigenous resources, even if this proved less economic than importation. On this issue Goering clashed with the industrialists and won; one of the monuments to his victory was the state-owned Hermann Goering works at Salzgitter, where low-grade ores were mined, as an alternative to importation of high-grade ores. Hitler never looked upon autarky as more than a temporary expedient; *Lebensraum* remained the only long-term solution to Germany's problems. Even if autarky had alleviated the difficulties of a peace-time economy, it could not solve those of war. On the eve of the invasion of Russia Hitler admitted as much: 'The course of the war shows that we have gone too far in our efforts to achieve autarky. It is impossible to produce all that we lack by synthetic

[3] *DGFP*, C, V, p.490

processes. . . . These strivings for autarky make great demands on manpower, which just cannot be met.'[4] Manpower was indeed the crux; although employment of forced labour from occupied countries began in 1940, it did not significantly affect production in that year; the expansion of the army necessary for the Russian campaign could only be achieved at the expense of industry.[5] Appeals were made for women volunteers, but in the autumn of 1940 only 300,000 more were employed than one year before. Sauckel's vicious slave raids in the occupied East, which did more than anything else to preclude civilian co-operation with the conquerors, were directly attributable to this continuing manpower shortage.

Nazi concern about civilian morale in a Reich from which freedom of expression had been banned led to the curious result that responsibility for reporting to the leadership on public opinion fell upon the SD, which was also responsible for preventing free discussion. The SD reports display unusual candour, so much so that in the latter phase of the war, when the truth had become even more unendurable to the war leaders, the reporting unit was suppressed.[6] Two main topics, apart from the natural public reaction to RAF raids, dominate the reports relating to the early war years: concern about supplies of rationed goods, and longing for an end to the war. At the end of January 1941, when Hitler made his annual speech to commemorate his coming to power, the general public noted the omission of any reference to relations with the USSR.[7] From that date until the invasion began the reports contain frequent references to popular anxiety about an extension of the war. Nazi leaders, who were well aware of the state of opinion, were determined to go on producing butter as well as guns. This had always been their attitude. In November 1938 Goering had refused to curtail production for the civil sector, even

[4] *Geschichte der Wehrwirtschaft*, op. cit., pp.300-1
[5] Ibid., p.240
[6] *Meldungen aus dem Reich*: ed. H. Boberach (Munich, 1968), p.29
[7] Ibid., p.133

though production of armaments suffered.[8] In 1941 more consumer goods were produced in the Reich than in 1940.[9] The attitude of Hitler and Goering was, of course, reflected by the *Gauleiters*, who on the outbreak of war became Defence Commissars in their areas. They stoutly opposed direction of labour,[10] and in defence of small business, in which the NSDAP had always been interested, they struggled against concentration of industry in the hands of larger, more efficient firms.[11]

Hitler's opposition to total war went further; he was determined not only that the people should have bread, in which they too were keenly interested, but he wanted them to have circuses. In the winter of 1939-40 work on the winter Olympics stadium at Garmisch in Bavaria continued.[12] In the summer of 1940 Hitler insisted that Speer's grandiose building projects for Berlin and Nuremberg should go ahead and an impressive allocation of scarce iron was made under a 'cover' name.[13] As late as mid-March 1942 Hitler had still not completely suspended work on beautifying Linz, which was to replace Vienna as Danube queen.[14] It was as if he were determined to go into his last great battle with one arm in a sling. As Professor Milward sums it up, perhaps with an understatement: 'No economic planning such as preceded the Anglo-American invasion of France preceded the German invasion of Russia.'[15]

'My Generals know nothing about the economic aspects of war,' observed Hitler;[16] but there was at least one who had made a thorough study of these aspects, and he disagreed with Hitler on almost every point. Georg Thomas, after serving under Beck in the Dresden military district, took up General Staff duties in 1928 on the economic

[8] *Design for Total War*, op. cit., p.159
[9] Ibid., p.229
[10] *Geschichte der Wehrwirtschaft*, op. cit., p.160
[11] *Design for Total War*, op. cit., p.205
[12] *Geschichte der Wehrwirtschaft*, op. cit., p.197
[13] *Inside the Third Reich*, op. cit., p.177
[14] *Deutschlands Ruestung*, op. cit., p.80
[15] *German Economy at War*: A. S. Milward (London, 1965), p.32
[16] *Panzer Leader*, op. cit., p.260

side and by November 1939 had become a Major-General in charge of the Office of War Economy and Armaments, which formed part of the OKW. There he remained till January 1943, when Keitel, in dismissing him, went on to say: 'I must concede to you today that your warnings and economic judgements before and during the war were correct. But you have made yourself intolerable to the Fuehrer and the Party by expressing these views loud and often. Hitler has made clear that he has no use for men who seek continually to instruct him.'[17] It is indicative of Hitler's reluctance to consider views that differed from his own that from 1940 to 1942 he received Thomas, who was his leading military expert on the economics of war, on only one occasion.[18] Since Thomas's criticisms were written down in the period of 18 months between his dismissal and his arrest, these can be taken as the genuine expression of views held at the time, rather than self-justification after the event, such as characterizes so much of the reminiscences of Hitler's Generals.

Thomas's basic disagreement with Hitler was over the latter's strategic concept of *Blitzkrieg* as a means of avoiding a lengthy war against a coalition of enemies. He believed that, in the end, Germany would again be ringed by foes and that, in particular, the underestimation of the might of the USA and USSR would prove fatal. He had visited the USSR in 1933 and had been 'deeply impressed with the vast expanse of Russian territory, the vitality of the people, the magnitude of their possibilities for self-sufficiency in raw materials and agricultural products, and especially the great dimensions of Russian industry . . .'[19] He had no confidence in autarky as a solution to Germany's economic problems. In any case, the risks of a long war should be met by three essential measures: first, the imposition of 'total war' restrictions on the civil sector; secondly, the introduction of a con-

---

[17] *Design for Total War*, op. cit., p.2
[18] *Geschichte der Wehrwirtschaft*, op. cit., p.200
[19] Ibid., p.45

sistent and rational system of priorities for allocation of arms contracts, manpower and raw materials; thirdly, rearmament in depth, so that the war machine rested on a solid infrastructure and plans could be made for the future in the confidence that these could be fulfilled, whether or not extra supplies of loot became available. Thomas claims to have advanced all these propositions 'with special emphasis before the beginning of the Russian campaign'.[20]

On the first point, we have already seen that Hitler wished at all cost to avoid total war on the home front. On the second, we saw in Chapter III that Hitler steadfastly refused to operate a co-ordinated system of military planning, or to link the military to the civil sector by administrative machinery. Goering, who fully shared Hitler's contempt for the General Staff and its cautious and methodical habits, had removed from the Army Ordnance Office the procurement for the Luftwaffe, in order to accelerate its expansion after 1933. The Navy and, in due course, the Waffen-SS followed suit. In 1938 a new competitor was introduced into the scramble for diminishing resources, manpower and foreign exchange, when Hitler, dissatisfied with the army's progress in the construction of the West Wall, placed the work in the independent hands of Fritz Todt, who had made his name building Germany's strategic roads. The Polish war, short as it was, showed that far more munitions and explosives were expended than had been foreseen.[21] Hitler's response was not to provide a clear answer to the question already posed by Thomas, namely whether he should expand production potential in preparation for a long war;[22] but to promote Todt in March 1940 to be Minister for Munitions and Weapons. As the armed forces were not instructed to place contracts through him, his appointment had the effect of introducing a new competitor, rather than supplanting existing ones.

[20] Ibid., p.159
[21] Ibid., p.177
[22] Ibid., p.171

Hitler was temperamentally averse from holding men or materials in reserve; the process by which a shell was produced and brought to the front-line did not interest him; it was the explosion and destruction that held his attention. He was therefore unresponsive to arguments in favour of arming in depth. There was, however, another, more rational explanation of his attitude, related to *Blitzkrieg* and its role in his master plan. We saw in Chapter IV that the flexibility of this long-term plan was one of its essential features; enemies were to be isolated and attacked in sequence, but the items in the sequence were interchangeable, as he had strikingly demonstrated in the summer of 1939. It followed that armament in depth, based on the assumption that Germany would fight one particular type of war, would eliminate Hitler's freedom of choice, by precluding a war of another kind. His answer to Thomas's enquiry at the end of September 1939 about long-term production plans had thus been that the arms industry must be ready to adapt rapidly to new situations.[23] Halder got a very similar reply at the end of August 1940, when Hitler had not finally made up his mind whether Sea Lion would be worth the risk, or whether to concentrate on Barbarossa: 'The army must be ready for everything, though no clear assignment of tasks is given.'[24] In Hitler's eyes, armament in breadth was the answer, because the impact of *Blitzkrieg* ensured that the war would be short.[25] The flaw in this argument was that the conditions obtaining on the Russian front did not lend themselves to *Blitzkrieg*; officers, like Thomas, who ventured to point this out, were simply accused of pessimism.

It was not until Hitler, with a lost war on his hands, was finally thrown on the defensive that rational, long-term priorities were fixed for the armed forces, with the result that production in the designated areas rose in 1943 and 1944, in spite of Anglo-American bombing. Thomas

23 Ibid.
24 *Halder/KTB*, II, p.79
25 *Design for Total War*, op. cit., pp.47-8

has charted the earlier vagaries. At the end of January 1939, when Hitler's antagonism to Britain was growing, priority was given to naval production.[26] In October 1939 priorities were revised with massive emphasis on attack: mobile forces for the army; U-boats for the Navy; dive-bombers for the Luftwaffe.[27] The decision to expand the army in the late summer of 1940 meant a further change; but this failed to take adequate account of the burden falling on the Luftwaffe, which had not only suffered heavily in the Battle of Britain, but was expected to divide its forces between the western and eastern fronts. As a result, only 61% of total combat aircraft could be deployed against Russia in June 1941.[28] Between 1939 and 1941 average monthly production of fighters had only risen from 183 to 244 and of bombers from 217 to 336. German producers were failing at this crucial stage to develop new types of aircraft. As Professor Milward puts it, 'It was not expected that the Russian war would last long enough to outdate any of the German aeroplanes.'[29] The same over-confidence meant that in February 1941 top priority had to be given to research and development, since it had become clear that in such areas as radar Germany was lagging behind. For the first time some emphasis had also to be placed on anti-aircraft defences.[30] An authoritative Luftwaffe estimate was that by 1943 the Anglo-American air forces combined would have a 5:1 advantage over the Germans.[31]

Two clear examples of failure to arm in depth may be cited. In one case, uncertainties about the war's duration and changing priorities led to a severe shortage of machine tools, without which rapid expansion of the industry could not be achieved. In mid-January 1940 Goering, alerted by Thomas, finally issued a directive in a letter describing production of machine tools as 'completely in-

[26] *Geschichte der Wehrwirtschaft*, op. cit., p.132
[27] Ibid., p.169
[28] *Hitlers Strategie*, op. cit., p.457
[29] *German Economy*, op. cit., p.137
[30] *Geschichte der Wehrwirtschaft*, op. cit., p.283
[31] Ibid., p.286

adequate'.[32] The second case was one in which insufficient attention to infrastructure had more dramatic results in the critical winter of 1941-2. The railways had no spokesman with direct access to Hitler and, although in August 1940 the OKW stressed the need to expand the system, the fatal assumption that the Russian war would be of short duration resulted in nothing being done.[33] In the spring of 1941, when the Balkan campaign coincided with the build-up for Barbarossa, civilian traffic in some areas almost came to a standstill and, because of inability to transport coal, industrial production was seriously affected.[34] Worse was to come in the bitter December of 1941, when the railways virtually came to a halt at the time of the failure to take Moscow, with the result that only 30% of the most vital consignments of arms and munitions could be moved.[35]

The classic instance of faulty planning combined with over-confidence is, of course, that of the army's winter clothing. Apart from the *Waffen*-SS, whose needs were met, provision was made for only one-fifth of the troops deployed, those who were to garrison the distant frontier after Russian resistance had collapsed.[36] To have provided for all would have led to pressure on the textile industry, and restrictions on the civilian sector. By August 1941 some sense of reality entered into military thinking and the NSDAP initiated the Winter Help programme of voluntary collection of clothing; but by that date the transport system could not cope with the additional burden. By November the German soldiers on the bleak Russian plains were trying to keep out the cold with clothing seized from the despised *Untermenschen*.

In 1939 the following were among the strategic raw materials on which the Reich was dependent on foreign suppliers for 50% or more of its needs: bauxite, copper,

[32] *OKW/KTB*, I, pp.957-8
[33] *Geschichte der Wehrwirtschaft*, op. cit., p.198
[34] Ibid., p.293
[35] Ibid., p.295
[36] *German General Staff*, op. cit., p.389

lead, nickel, oil, rubber and tin.[37] It was only the assurance of supply of these and other commodities, including food, from and through Russia that had allowed Hitler to embark on war against the Western Powers. Seizure of stocks in countries occupied in 1940 had improved his immediate prospects; but it was only possible to exploit the armaments industries of occupied countries if, as in the case of France, coal and oil was made available.[38] Moreover, these additional resources were cancelled out by the demands of existing allies, such as Italy, which was without indigenous supplies of oil and coal, and new allies, such as Finland and Romania, which required to be supplied with arms for the coming campaign against the USSR. Even neutral Turkey was able to drive a hard bargain, because of Germany's dependence upon Turkish chrome.[39]

War had somewhat alleviated the Reich's perennial difficulty in paying for its imports; but it had not solved the problem of reconciling exports with the imperative demands of home production both for the Wehrmacht and for the home market. In any case there was a more fundamental conundrum facing the economic planners in the late autumn of 1940: how was Germany to conquer Russia without the raw materials supplied by Russia under existing agreements? In order to arrive at a plausible answer, it was necessary to assume not only a short war, but also remarkable success in seizing intact major sectors of Soviet industry and securing the co-operation of Soviet industrial and agricultural workers. Goering made these assumptions without question when early in November 1940 he instructed Thomas to be prepared for a longer war,[40] and then went on to speak of the exploitation of Soviet industrial installations in the Ukraine.[41] Thomas's investigations induced in him an even heavier

[37] *Geschichte der Wehrwirtschaft*, op. cit., pp.146-7
[38] Ibid., p.222
[39] Ibid., p.281
[40] *OKW/KTB*, I, p.168
[41] *Bergbau u. Eisenhuetten Industrie in d. Ukraine*: M. Riedel in *VfZg*, Munich, 1973

depression than usual; he saw that transportation was the key factor and, therefore, that oil and rubber were the weakest points. On 8 February 1941 he discussed these commodities with Keitel and, in order to procure rubber, they debated the desperate expedient of running the blockade.[42] Three days later he calculated that, if there were no imports after the end of March 1941, production of rubber at an inadequate level could continue for 8 months, after which only buna would be available.[43]

As regards mineral oil, over two-fifths of Germany's vital imports had come from Russia in 1940.[44] Thomas now reckoned that the Wehrmacht had enough aviation fuel to last till the autumn of 1941, but that fuel for vehicles would only last till mid-August 1941.[45] This gloomy report obliged Goering to demand a renewed appraisal, as a result of which Thomas reaffirmed his view that success in a war of short duration would depend on preventing destruction of enemy stores, seizing the oil-producing areas of the Caucasus without demolitions, and solving the transport problem. For a longer war, not only would these conditions have to be fulfilled, but it would also be necessary to induce the population to co-operate. Even so, unless links with the Far East could be re-established, there could be no solution to the problem of securing adequate supplies of rubber, wolfram, copper, platinum, tin, asbestos and hemp.[46]

No serious attempt was made either to dispute these conclusions, or to reassess the invasion decision. It is true that early in March Goering discussed with Thomas the possibility of using parachute troops to seize Baku, but the Luftwaffe General Staff, when consulted, expressed ignorance of the project.[47] In any case, Goering's decision to use these elite troops in the costly attack on Crete administered a crippling blow to their strength. As re-

[42] *OKW/KTB*, I, p.313
[43] Ibid., p.317
[44] *Geschichte der Wehrwirtschaft*, op. cit., p.254
[45] *OKW/KTB*, I, p.317
[46] *Geschichte der Wehrwirtschaft*, op. cit., p.268
[47] *OKW/KTB*, I, p.349

gards the Far Eastern link, Goering concluded that the trans-Siberian railway could be reopened with Japanese co-operation.[48] Yet nothing further was done until on 28 June 1941, after the invasion had begun, Ribbentrop instructed the German Embassy in Tokio to influence the Japanese in favour of 'speedy military action against the Soviet Union'.[49] Hitler failed to support the demarche of his Foreign Minister until mid-July, by which time the Japanese had taken the vital decision to turn south and the Cabinet was about to be reshuffled omitting Matsuoka (see Chapter XI).

Thomas's report would have led any responsible leadership either to abandon plans of aggression or, at least, to select less ambitious objectives. Whilst it cannot be stated with certainty that Hitler actually saw the report, he seems to have registered one point, which indeed had been in his mind since July 1940, namely that the Wehrmacht would have to get to the Russian oilfields. This increased his interest in the task allotted to Army Group South and at a critical point in the campaign exacerbated a defect already inherent in the strategic plan, which provided that (to quote Guderian), 'three Army Groups . . . were to attack with diverging objectives'.[50] Hitler was thus led late in July 1941 to divert forces from the thrust against Moscow which, after the fall of Kiev on 20 September 1941, was resumed too late in the year to have prospect of success.[51]

Goering, who should have been primarily responsible for impressing upon Hitler the economic risks he was incurring, seems to have made no effort to do so. Only Weizsaecker in a memorandum to Ribbentrop of 28 April 1941 made a last minute attempt to bring home some of the implications: 'If every burnt-out Russian town were worth as much to us as an English ship sunk, then I would favour German-Russian war this summer;

---

[48] *IMT*, XXVII, 1157-PS
[49] *DGFP*, D, 13, p.40
[50] *Panzer Leader*, op. cit., p.142
[51] *The Russo-German War:* op. cit., pp.142-3

but I believe that against Russia we shall only lose economically what we gain militarily . . . I take it for granted that militarily we shall press forward victoriously to Moscow and beyond. But I very much doubt whether we can exploit what we have conquered against the well known passive resistance of the Slav.'[52] Hitler ignored these views, as well as those of Rosenberg, who observed to his staff on 20 June 1941 that 'it makes a difference whether after a few years I win over 40 million men to voluntary co-operation, or whether a soldier has to stand behind every peasant'.[53] How Hitler ensured that soldiers would have to deal not only with peasants, but with armed partisans is the theme of the next chapter.

[52] *Das Dritte Reich im Kreuzverhoer:* R. M. W. Kempner (Munich, 1969), pp.232-3
[53] *IMT*, Vol. XXVI, 1058-PS

# X

# Barbarossa: Political Planning

In the strange story of Hitler's plans to invade Russia nothing is stranger than the almost complete neglect of those methods of political and psychological warfare, about which he had so often written and spoken and which he had effectively practised against other enemies since 1938 – or since 1934, if one takes into account the abortive putsch in Austria in the summer of that year. If there is one chapter of *Mein Kampf* that retains objective interest, apart from what is revealed about the author himself, it is Chapter VI, containing shrewd observations on 'War Propaganda'. We have frequently noted that the First World War made a deep impression on Hitler's mind; he excoriated the ineptitude of German propaganda and admired the excellence of Britain's, which had not only undermined 'the stamina of our people at home',[1] but had also infected the armed forces, a point which he illustrated by citing the influence of British anti-Prussian propaganda upon the Bavarian troops with whom he served. He ascribed the November Revolution in part to the cumulative effect of *Entente* propaganda. Though he did not refer to it in *Mein Kampf*, he was well aware of the devastating effect produced in Russia by the German General Staff's most important act of psychological warfare, namely the transportation of Lenin from Switzerland to Russia, which he discussed with Rosenberg in 1921.[2]

Hitler drew two main conclusions from this part of his wartime experience, one relating to the home front and one to the war of nerves against the enemy. In the domestic field he was determined, as we saw in the last chapter, to prevent a repetition of the 1918 collapse by maintaining as long as possible a reasonable standard of living. As he said to Rauschning, his government must

[1] *Mein Kampf*, op. cit., p.162
[2] *Lagebesprechungen*, op. cit., pp.114-15

'never be associated with measures that had once already plunged the Reich into misery and defeat'.[3] Elimination of ideologically unreliable and racially 'impure' elements would reinforce this precaution. As far as external enemies were concerned, he aimed to sow among them confusion and dissension, which at the critical moment would be converted into panic and, if possible, submission by use of rumour, 'black' radio transmissions and other sophisticated techniques of subversion. As he said to Rauschning, war would not be waged by him 'solely as a military operation . . .[4] Our strategy is to destroy the enemy from within.'[5] This formed part of the strategy of *Blitzkrieg*, as applied to the civilian population.

National minorities within enemy states were a special target, such as the Irish in Britain and the Flemings in Belgium. This was not, in fact, an innovation of the Second World War, though the use of radio made exploitation of such groups easier than in the First. The German General Staff, whose capacity for political warfare Hitler so much despised, had effectively exploited particularist tendencies in Russia, and had concluded a separate peace treaty with the Ukraine early in February 1918 after Trotsky had at first refused to sign. After the Treaty of Brest-Litovsk had finally been signed, the particularist policy in the Ukraine broke down, because the German occupying forces under Field-Marshal v. Eichhorn, in their efforts to draw on the economic potential of the province, only succeeded (to quote Gen. Hoffmann) 'in driving the Ukraine back into the arms of Great Russia'.[6] The heir to this policy in the NSDAP was Rosenberg, who seemed in the late 1920s to have made a convert of Hitler. In 1931 the latter was reported as having described Russia as 'a heterogeneous conglomeration of peoples, differing in language and characteristics'.[7] Three years later Hitler, in conversation with Rauschning, envisaged a Great German Reich, controlling 'an alliance of

[3] *Hitler Speaks*, op. cit., p.207
[4] Ibid., pp.211-12
[5] Ibid., p.18
[6] *Forgotten Peace*, op. cit., p.324

vassal states', which was to include Poland, the Baltic States, Hungary, the Balkans, the Ukraine, the Volga basin and Georgia.[8] The whole concept evidently rested upon the need to show at least a minimum of respect for the semi-autonomous regions, whose ethnic and cultural differences were to be used for German imperial ends.

The attractions of such a policy for bringing about the disintegration of the USSR had been greatly increased since 1918 by the advent of Stalinism. Whilst it was still possible to appeal over the heads of the Muscovite 'Great Russians' to the particularism of Georgians, Cossacks, Tatars and others, it had also become possible to exploit the deep discontents brought about by Stalin's ruthless autocracy. The rigid controls of his police state could not altogether conceal from the outside world the liquidation of the *Kulaks* and the purges in the Red Army. Because the Red Army recruited most of its soldiers among the peasantry, these measures had combined to affect morale. Hitler was presented with an exceptional opportunity to practise political warfare against the USSR; he could pose not only as the liberator of the lesser nationalities, which had never been permitted to benefit from the original Soviet self-determination decree of November 1917, but he could also free all Russians from other unpopular measures of Bolshevism, such as collectivization of agriculture and the forcible suppression of religion.

When Hitler first spoke to his Generals in July 1940 about the political objectives of the Russian campaign (see p.75) he encouraged the assumption that he intended to create a ring of subservient protectorates to cordon off Great Russia, along the lines indicated in his conversation with Rauschning in 1934. Staff officers proceeded accordingly; early in September 1940 Jodl issued instructions to the *Abwehr* to 'use its agents for kindling national antagonism among the people of the USSR'.[9] Lossberg in his strategic study wrote, 'Once the Ukraine is occu-

[7] *Myth of Master Race*, op. cit., p.169
[8] *Hitler Speaks*, op. cit., p.128
[9] *IMT*, VII, p.272

pied a 'Government' responsive to our wishes will probably be formed. This will ease the task of supervising the extensive occupied areas.'[10] The *Abwehr* actually continued to assume, even after the invasion of Russia had begun, that the separatist policy was in force; it had for several years supported an Organization of Ukrainian Nationalists (OUN), leadership of which was taken over after the collapse of Poland by the Ukrainian activist, Stephen Bandera, who had been imprisoned by the Poles. At the end of June 1941, soon after Lvov in Galicia had been captured by the invaders, Bandera and other OUN leaders set up a provisional Ukrainian regime there, backed by the Uniate Church, which was associated with provincial nationalism, in opposition to the Orthodox Church with its spiritual home in Moscow. On orders from Berlin the regime was promptly suppressed and Bandera removed to the Reich.[11] As an added blow to Ukrainian aspirations, Galicia was at the beginning of August 1941 turned over to the tyrannical administration of the Government-General of Poland.

That the belief should have persisted in military circles that Hitler might be prepared to use some Slavs to fight other Slavs shows how little his ideological attitude was understood, even by those serving him. It is true that in January 1939, when he was toying with the idea of doing a deal with Poland, he had remarked that, 'Every Polish Division that fights against Russia saves one German Division.'[12] But later that year his policy in occupied Poland had excluded any such possibility. The Polish bourgeoisie, among whom some collaborators against Bolshevism might have been found, was the special object of the genocidal activities of the SS; the working class was condemned to slave labour. Only the *Abwehr* profited by their opportunity to employ Polish agents against the USSR.[13] The rest of the population was left with no

[10] *German Strategy against Russia*, op. cit., App. II
[11] *DGFP*, D, XIII, p.156
[12] *Sonderakte Barbarossa*, op. cit., p.39
[13] *IMT*, VII, pp.262-3

alternative between resistance and abject submission. In October 1940, when even Hans Frank pointed out that deportations and depredations were making the Government-General no longer viable, Hitler replied that survival of Poles was a matter of indifference to him.[14] It was exactly the attitude he was later to adopt towards the people of the Ukraine; as he said in 1942 to Bormann, who had been distressed during a drive through the Ukrainian countryside to see so many healthy children, 'We must take all the measures necessary to ensure that the non-German population does not increase at an excessive rate . . . it would be sheer folly to place at their disposal a health service . . .'[15]

It was not until the beginning of December 1940, when preparations for Barbarossa were well advanced and other options foreclosed, that Hitler began to show his hand by speaking in terms that seemed to preclude a traditional political termination of the war (see p.125). He made himself clearer early in March 1941, when he rejected the OKW's draft directive providing for military administration in the territory to be occupied, on the ground that the army would be incapable of solving the political problems with which it would be faced. His true motive emerged, however, in his insistence that Himmler's henchmen would be responsible for liquidating the 'Jewish-Bolshevik intelligentsia', as well as 'Bolshevik bosses and commissars'.[16] Two days later he expressed himself more guardedly to Halder: 'The army would not be burdened with the administration. Special task for *Reichsfuehrer* SS.'[17] But with the example of Poland before him Halder can hardly have been in doubt what was intended. The OKW in revising their draft directive made some effort to avert the enormities that Hitler had enjoined; the new text made no explicit mention of the groups to be liquidated, but merely referred to the 'special tasks' assigned to

[14] *National-Sozialistische Polenpolitik:* M. Broszat (Munich, 1965), p.27
[15] *Hitler's Table Talk*, op. cit., p.588
[16] *OKW/KTB*, I, p.341
[17] *Halder KTB*, II, p.303

Himmler in rear areas, in connection with 'the final struggle of two opposed political systems'.[18] The OKH accepted the directive, as signed by Keitel, and General Wagner, the Quarter-Master General, discussed with Heydrich the role of the 'Special Commandos' in the future area of operations.[19]

The attitude of most army officers at this stage seems to have been one of resignation in the face of the atrocities contemplated, provided that they were not directly involved. Hitler, however, had every intention of making them his partners in crime. He dispersed all illusions at a meeting on 30 March 1941 of over 200 senior officers of the Wehrmacht; he placed outside the normal rules of war, which had been observed in previous campaigns, not only the two categories of Communists already mentioned, but all indigenous inhabitants opposing the Wehrmacht, who were to be shot out of hand; military courts were expressly excluded. It was to be, Hitler insisted, a battle of annihilation; 'the reconstitution of an educated class (*Intelligenz*) must be prevented'.[20]

It might have been expected that this instruction, which was to be translated into the infamous 'Commissar order' addressed to Commanding Officers, would have aroused some objections. Quite apart from any humanitarian considerations, it was calculated to intensify resistance, preclude the collaboration of the inhabitants and provoke reprisals against Wehrmacht prisoners. There is no evidence that any voice was raised at the conference; nor did Halder, who occasionally implied a criticism, if the Fuehrer slighted the army, record any in his diary. His account of this part of the conference concludes with the laconic note: 'Midday: luncheon together.'[21] Some of those present, including Bock, were influenced by the fact that the USSR had not signed the Geneva Convention on the rules of war.[22] Five years after the begin-

[18] *Im Hauptquartier*, op. cit., p.170
[19] Ibid., pp.173-4
[20] *Halder KTB*, II, p.336
[21] Ibid.
[22] *Gegen Hitler u. Stalin*, op. cit., p.22

ning of the invasion Rundstedt was cross-examined in Nuremberg by Dr Kempner, a former German civil servant and refugee from Nazism, who was attached to the US Prosecutor; he tried to extract from the Field-Marshal the admission that he and his colleagues could have influenced Hitler's decisions and need not have acted like 'a corps of postmen'. Kempner's attempt failed; Rundstedt, even after the shame and tragedy of 1945, was not to be shifted one centimetre from the classic formulation of the role of the 'non-political' soldier: 'The political aspect does not concern the officer; he carries out the military duty assigned to him by his superior.'[23] The Marshals and Generals had been cowed by Hitler; but they were also the victims of their own military tradition.

It remained for the OKH and OKW to agree upon a directive embodying Hitler's instructions. Warlimont has claimed that he was reluctant to comply, but that Wagner pointed out that failure to do so would only result in SD Special Commandos coming into the front line to execute their grisly tasks. At this juncture an unforeseen ally emerged in the unlikely person of Rosenberg, who had independently stressed to Hitler that Soviet officials would be required for civil administration and that the proposed victimization should be confined to the senior ones.[24] The directive was issued early in June on this basis; but propaganda leaflets prepared for distribution behind Red Army lines were not modified. Shortly before the invasion one of these came into the hands of Wilfried Strik-Strikfeldt, a former Tsarist officer, who since the Russian Revolution had made his career in Germany and had been attached as interpreter and liaison officer to Bock's HQ. He was appalled to read the exhortation to the Russian civilians to co-operate with their 'liberators' by killing not only Commissars, but all members of the Communist Party, including its youth movement (*Komsomol*). It was at once plain to him that the leaflet would not only provoke fanatical resistance, but would stand no more chance

[23] *Reich im Kreuzverhoer*, op. cit., p.87
[24] *Im Hauptquartier*, op. cit., pp.180-1: *IMT*, XXVI, 884-PS

of being carried out than would a parallel appeal to the German people to join with Russian invaders in slaughtering members of the Hitler Youth.[25] Bock agreed and was successful in having reference to Party and *Komsomol* members removed from the leaflets; but since the SD adhered to their own instructions, this modification had only a short-term impact, if any.

We have dealt at length with the Commissar order, because it so clearly illustrates Hitler's determination, even before battle was joined, to fight a war of an ideological character, whatever the disadvantages in military terms. The same point is emphasized by the fact that, until the end of March 1941, his instructions for civil administration had, with the exception of one sentence in the OKW directive, been confined to the liquidation of certain categories of his enemies. The OKW directive had specified the rear areas of the three Army Groups (Baltic area, White-Russia and Ukraine) and made provision for these to be administered by Reich Commissioners 'who will receive their instructions from the Fuehrer'.[26] Something more was evidently needed and Hitler summoned Rosenberg and told him to draw up proposals. Rosenberg had been regarded as the leading Eastern expert of the NSDAP before the Party came to power, but had been shown very few favours since; his appointment in April 1941 to head a Bureau for the Central Handling of Questions of the East European Area[27] has therefore puzzled historians. Alexander Dallin has expressed the view that the decision was motivated by Bormann, who 'preferred a crack-brained *Ostminister* to a clever one . . .'[28] Crack-brained he may have been, but he showed himself a good deal less so than Hitler and Bormann, who persisted in their anti-Slav policies beyond the point of no return.

Rosenberg, who now moved for the first time from the

[25] *Gegen Hitler u. Stalin*, op. cit., pp.13-14
[26] *Im Hauptquartier*, op. cit., p.170
[27] DGFP, D, XIII, pp.28-9
[28] *German Rule in Russia*: A. Dallin (London, 1957), p.35

NSDAP hierarchy into that of the State, recommended that he be interposed as Minister between Hitler and the Reich Commissioners, whose number was first increased to seven and then reduced to four: *Ostland* (Baltic area); Ukraine; Caucasus and Moscow.[29] In the event only Commissioners for the first two areas were appointed, namely *Gauleiters* Lohse and Koch. Whilst all the rigours of Nazi ideology were to be imposed on the Great Russians in the Muscovite area, the other three regions were to receive more favourable treatment, though not uniformly so; the main task of the Minister would be to preserve these graduations, in so far as this proved consistent with the economic needs of the Reich.

This latter proviso was in accord with Rosenberg's own views, but was in any case imposed by Goering, whose Economic Control Staff East was solely concerned with exploitation of the occupied areas, and accepted with equanimity that this would mean the death of many of the inhabitants.[30] Since security had also been removed from Rosenberg's field of responsibility, it is plain that his Ministry could not have done much to ameliorate the lot of the Russian population once the immediate onrush of *Blitzkrieg* had come to a halt and the Germans, in order to keep the war going, were in desperate need of additional human and material resources. None the less, a serious attempt to give substance to Rosenberg's proposals, together with humane treatment of civilians and prisoners of war, as in the First World War, would have lent plausibility to the image of 'Hitler the Liberator' and could have had an important effect on Soviet resistance in the first critical weeks. Alexander Dallin has summed it up as follows: 'There is little doubt that a skilful effort to win the population, civilian and military alike, to oppose the Soviet regime could have yielded substantial, and during the first months of the war perhaps decisive, results.'[31]

[29] *IMT*, XXVI, 1017-PS, 1019-PS
[30] *IMT*, XXVII, 1157-PS
[31] *German Rule in Russia,* op. cit., p.64

When Rosenberg prepared his plan, he had no reason to believe that Hitler had no intention of allowing him to carry it into effect; indeed on 30 March 1941 the Fuehrer at his conference with Wehrmacht leaders had referred to setting up 'protectorates in the Baltic countries, Ukraine and White Russia'. But he had significantly added, 'The new states must be socialist states, but without an indigenous educated class.'[32] A satellite state with which the Third Reich wished to co-operate would have been placed under an authoritarian figure, like the Ukrainian Hetman, Paul Skoropadski, in 1918; the protectorates were to be given socialist regimes not because these would be congenial to the inhabitants, but because, in Hitler's eyes, such regimes would be unstable and ineffectual, as the Weimar Republic had been. As usual, he was interested in submission, not in co-operation.

Rosenberg, who for the next two years persisted half-heartedly in trying to bring in measures of religious tolerance and redistribution of collectivized farms, calculated to appeal to the populace, seems never to have grasped this fundamental point. At the decisive conference in mid-July 1941 at Angersburg, at which his appointment as Minister was agreed (though only announced four months later), Rosenberg was still speaking in terms of Germany's traditional mission as bringer of culture to the benighted Slavs: 'In the Ukraine we should start with attention to cultural matters; there we ought to awaken the historical consciousness of the Ukrainians, establish a university at Kiev, and the like.' Goering merely commented that the first thought must be where food for Germany was coming from; everything else could wait.[33] Needless to say, Rosenberg not only failed to get his university, but had a hard task even keeping open primary schools in occupied Russia.

This was the root of his second basic error; he had not realized that the role of the Third Reich in the East was not to bring culture, but to prevent it from ever arising

---

[32] *Halder KTB*, II, p.336
[33] *DGFP*, D, XIII, p.149

there again. Hitler's true delegate in the East was Himmler, not Rosenberg, whose appointment must be regarded as something of a stalking-horse for the bemusement of those who still supposed that the Russian war was to be fought in a traditional way for rational ends. Staff of the Reich Commissar for Reinforcing Germandom (RKFDV) had begun work in 1940 on the *'Generalplan Ost'*, though it was not submitted to Himmler till May 1942.[34] It envisaged settlements of privileged soldier-peasants, dominating such indigenous inhabitants as remained to do menial work; but many of the latter were to be eliminated including all the Jews and gypsies and one quarter of the Russians.[35] These were to be replaced – since for many years there had been little enthusiasm for eastward emigration in Germany itself – by ethnic Germans from Hungary, Romania, Slovenia, the Tyrol and elsewhere.[36] The monstrous nature of these plans was not fully known, of course, until after the war; but a sufficient start was made on the elimination programme to show the trend. In addition, Himmler opposed parcelling out 'liberated' collective farms to the Russian peasantry, because it was necessary to hold large estates in reserve for the fortified homesteads of the *Herrenmenschen*.

At the end of June 1942 Hitler was musing after lunch in the 'Wolf's Lair' on the remarkable fighting spirit displayed by the Red Army, who 'fought like animals to the last breath and had to be finished off man by man'; it was not at all like 1916-17, when the Russians had struck their rifles muzzle downward in their trenches and evacuated their positions.[37] Nobody had the courage to tell the Fuehrer that he and his political henchmen were directly responsible for this enhanced resistance. There is abundant evidence that in many places the German army was at first welcomed, as it had been in 1917-18; Red Army

[34] *Generalplan Ost:* H. Heiber in *VfZg*, Munich, 1958
[35] *German Rule in Russia*, op. cit., p.299
[36] *RKFDV*, op. cit., p.227
[37] *Tischgespraeche*, op. cit., p.201

units, which had been cut off from the main body, surrendered readily. By the end of October 1941 no fewer than two million prisoners were in German hands; in the great encirclement battle of Kiev alone the Germans took 450,000.[38] But no proper provision was made for them; in the bitter cold of winter they were dying at the rate of 2,500 a day, so that Rosenberg was moved, if not by humane, then at least by political, considerations, to depict the situation to Hitler.[39] The Fuehrer remained unmoved; his attitude had been shown when he decided early in July 1941 not to take Leningrad, but to liquidate the population by starvation and bombardment. The Russians never forgot that in the winter of 1941-2 some 300,000 people died in Leningrad of hunger and cold. Over three million Soviet prisoners of war died in German hands; at least seven million civilians died in Russia.

In Smolensk the advancing Germans seized the NKVD records and found in them lists of Russians who had been prisoners in Germany in the First World War; these men had been objects of suspicion because they had been well treated and had not believed communist propaganda about the 'Fascist beasts'.[40] Now they and their families and friends were forced to accept as true what the Commissars had always said. Stalin was quick to exploit the failure of the Germans to draw any clear distinction between the anti-communist and anti-Slav characteristics of the so-called crusade; he exhorted the Russian people to join in 'The Great Patriotic War' and created new military orders bearing the names of the national heroes of earlier centuries, Suvorov and Kutusov.[41] Church bells, which in Germany were being melted down, began to swing again in Mother Russia. When early in July 1941 Stalin called for partisan warfare behind the German lines, Hitler welcomed it as a pretext 'to exterminate everyone who opposes us'.[42] The SD were quick to take

---

[38] *Russo-German War*, op. cit., p.146
[39] *IMT*, XXVII, 1517-PS
[40] *Gegen Hitler u. Stalin*, op. cit., p.18
[41] Ibid., p.58
[42] *DGFP*, D, XIII, p.149

reprisals and the villagers soon found themselves in
double jeopardy; even so partisan activity had not become a major threat to the German occupation at the end
of 1941.[43]

Hitler was radically opposed to Rosenberg's theory,
which was also espoused by most of the military leaders,
that Russia could only be defeated with the help of Slavs.
Hitler, apart from his ideological prejudice, was much
influenced by the experience of Ludendorff, who in the
First World War had advocated political concessions to
the Poles in the hope, which was disappointed, of raising
a Polish Legion.[44] Hitler was prepared to entrust arms
only to Moslems and on one occasion engaged his Chief
of Staff, who might have been better employed, in a con-
fused discussion as to whether the Georgians were a
Turkish people.[45] His Generals, who were not much
interested in the ethnic and cultural distinctions between
peoples, were in dire need of auxiliaries and by the end of
1941 had enlisted the services, as non-combatants, of
nearly one million volunteers in the occupied eastern
territories.[46] As German casualties grew, so did the temptation to arm these units and employ them against the
partisans; by 1943, when Hitler insisted on the removal
of these units from the eastern front, over 600,000 men
were serving under Koestring.[47] Not until 1944, when the
shortage of manpower was desperate, could Hitler be
finally persuaded to allow the Russian Liberation Army
to be formed under the renegade Russian General Vlasov.
That so much co-operation was forthcoming, in spite of
the crude brutality of the 'master race' and its ideology, is
an indication of the important role that political warfare
could have played, if organized with restraint – and even
compassion.

Co-operation with the civilian population, especially in
the southern part of the USSR, would certainly have

[43] *Russo-German War*, op. cit., p.221
[44] *Lagebesprechungen*, op. cit., p.113
[45] Ibid., pp.45-6
[46] *Gegen Hitler u. Stalin*, op. cit., p.45
[47] *House Built on Sand*, op. cit., p.354

presented little problem, if the Germans had been permitted by Hitler to fight a real war of liberation, instead of the ruthless colonial war that was characterized by Erich Koch's denunciation of the Ukrainian people as 'white niggers'.[48] Even as it was, whole groups, such as the Don Cossacks, who had a Central Cossack Office in Berlin, came over to the Germans.[49] Late in 1941 the Chechen-Ingushi and Karachai rebelled against Soviet rule before the German armies had reached their borders. The North Caucasian area, which they inhabited, lay outside the scope of Himmler's resettlement plans and, as they were not Slavs, there was less prejudice against them. For the short period of German occupation they were under direct military rule and were spared the savageries of the SS.[50] But not those of Stalin; after the war they, together with the Krim Tatars, Kalmyks, Volga Germans, and other entire ethnic groups, accused of collaboration with the invaders, were deported by Stalin from their homelands. There can be little doubt that a serious effort to detach the Ukraine, as in 1918, could have succeeded, at least temporarily. Instead, *Gauleiter* Fritz Sauckel was appointed in February 1942 to round up forced labour for the Reich. This provided an ideal opportunity for the sadistic Reich Commissioner; in October 1942 Koch closed all the secondary schools, so that the teachers, including women, and even pupils over 15 could be press-ganged into German labour camps.[51]

After the war Manstein correctly defined Hitler's basic error: 'while his strategic policy was to demolish the Soviet system with the utmost dispatch, his political actions were diametrically opposed to this.'[52] It is, if anything, an understatement; it could equally well be said that Hitler and Himmler were Stalin's staunchest allies. The so-called crusade against Bolshevism, so far from overthrowing the Soviet dictator, gave him the chance to

[48] *Myth of Master Race*, op. cit., p.198
[49] *German Rule in Russia*, op. cit., pp.329-31
[50] Ibid., pp.238-43
[51] *United States National Archives*, EAP 99/110 (microfilm)
[52] *Lost Victories*, op. cit., p.176

identify himself with the deepest instinct of the Russian people – that of national self-protection. He thus emerged immeasurably strengthened from the war and continued until his death in 1953 to subject his people to a secret police tyranny, of which Himmler would have been in no way ashamed.

# XI

## Ideologies in Mortal Combat

*Tantum religio potuit suadere malorum* – and it is true, too, of ideologies, both Fascist and Marxist, that in their name terrible things have been done. We may claim in the preceding chapters to have sufficiently shown that Hitler's fixed intention to attack Russia was based upon certain preconceived ideas of a racial and historical character; that he continued in this intention despite evidence that, in doing so, he would expose the German people to the greatest peril; and that the Russian war, when it came, was fought not in the way most likely to lead to victory, but in the manner most consistent with Hitler's ideological preconceptions. If this conclusion is accepted, the question when Hitler arrived at the decision to invade Russia is of only marginal relevance to our theme. Hitler had intended to bring about the destruction of the USSR from the time that he identified Moscow as the headquarters of the 'Judaeo-Bolshevist world conspiracy'. As he was a politician, as well as a fanatic, he was, of course, prepared to await the most favourable moment to carry out his plan of aggression; this appeared to occur in the summer of 1940, when he found himself – rather sooner than he had expected – the master of Europe. If at that point he had been logistically prepared for the invasion of Britain, or if Britain by capitulating had saved him the trouble, he could then have concentrated upon his eastern campaign with much improved prospects of success and, probably, with more whole-hearted co-operation on the part of his senior staff officers. Since these preconditions were not forthcoming, Hitler compensated by trying first to convince himself, and those around him, that Britain was, in effect, a defeated power, and then that the campaign in Russia could be swiftly brought to an end before the British, with American help, were on their feet again.

We have seen how Hitler, in seeking to justify his decision, especially in the presence of those who doubted its wisdom, made use of two barely compatible arguments, both leading to the same conclusion in favour of an early invasion of Russia. One was that Germany should take advantage of Russia's weakness, since victory would be quick and relatively easy; the other was that Russia's potential strength was so immense that, unless she was at once attacked and destroyed, she would inevitably destroy Germany. Once the campaign had begun, despite the sensational successes of the opening weeks, no more was heard of the first argument; as the difficulties of the campaign grew, the second argument developed into the claim that Hitler had been forced into fighting a preventive war, in order to save the German people from a worse fate. He had known all along, even if he had not been willing to admit it, that the invasion was a gamble. He began to see very soon after it started that the odds against him were longer than he had reckoned.

It is in this light that one should read the record of Hitler's conversation with Oshima on 14 July 1941. Less than one week after the invasion had begun Ribbentrop had sent off two telegrams to Ott designed to induce the Japanese to take 'speedy military action against the Soviet Union'.[1] He followed these up by a personal message to Matsuoka on 1 July 1941, affirming in emphatic terms that, 'The need of the hour is for the Japanese Army to seize Vladivostok as soon as possible and penetrate as deeply toward the West as possible.'[2] In other words, he recognized that Germany might, after all, be in for a long war; for this, he wrote after the war, he was severely reproached by Hitler.[8] Yet barely two weeks later Hitler himself was hinting to Oshima that the hour for Japanese intervention had struck. Germany and Japan, he said, must join together to destroy the USSR and USA; he did not, of course, need Japanese help, but was speaking in

[1] *DGFP*, D, XIII, p.40
[2] Ibid., p.61
[8] *Ribbentrop Memoirs*, op. cit., p.159

this sense to Oshima in Japan's own interest, since only
the elimination of the USSR would keep the USA out of
the war. It is an echo of the earlier argument that Russia
must be destroyed so that Britain would see the need to
capitulate. Hitler emphasized that, 'In broad terms the
Russian army was already beaten;' but he also admitted
that the Wehrmacht had met with 'a series of great sur-
prises', including giant tanks.[4] His words, as we saw in
Chapter VII, fell upon deaf ears.

One week later Hitler received 'Marshal' Kvaternik,
the puppet dictator of Croatia, to whom he related the
economic version of the preventive war; 'The plans of the
Kremlin were now clear. In the autumn the Bolsheviks
would first have occupied the Romanian oilwells and
turned off our oil supplies, without our being in the position to do anything about it. At the same time they
would have attacked Finland and cut us off from the
nickel . . .'[5] Gradually the legend of preventive war took
shape, much as the 'stab in the back' legend had been
built up after the First World War. On 3 October 1941,
when Hitler, though still claiming that the war had been
won, was leading the appeal for winter clothing for the
Wehrmacht on the Russian front, he described the decision to invade as 'the hardest decision of my whole life
up to that time'. But there had been no escape from it:
'Already in May the situation was so threatening that
there could no longer be any doubt that Russia intended
to fall upon us at the first opportunity.'[6]

Hitler knew very well that this was a travesty of the
facts. He did not have to accept the evidence of Stalin's
clumsy gestures towards the German Embassy in Moscow,
nor of the reassuring and anti-Western Tass communiqué
of 14 June 1941, which the press in the Reich was not
allowed to publish.[7] Hitler, who preferred devious sources
of information, had a better one: at some point before

---

[4] *Staatsmaenner*, op. cit., pp.293-301
[5] Ibid., pp.304-5
[6] *Reden u. Proklamationen*, Vol. II, p.1762
[7] *Incompatible Allies*, op. cit., p.335

the invasion the Germans had secured access to texts of certain telegrams of guidance on current Soviet policy sent to Soviet Missions in the Far East. On 7 May 1941 these Missions were informed that the USSR was trying to avert friction with Germany in connection with Turkey and the Near East. On 11 May they were told that it was the Soviet intention to share out spheres of interest with Germany and Italy – a clear indication that Stalin had not given up hope that the negotiations initiated with Molotov in November 1940 might before long be resumed. This piece of information may, on reflection, have seemed rather bald, because ten days later it was followed by another telegram explaining that the USSR had no sympathy with the imperialism of Germany and Japan, but was using it in order to destroy the imperialism of England and America. Consistently with this guidance, a further telegram was sent on 3 June 1941, foreseeing a worsening of relations with the two Anglo-Saxon countries and the need to foment unrest in them.[8] It must have been clear to Hitler that, whether or not the Anglo-Saxons were his prime enemies, they were certainly Stalin's. The master-plan of the Soviet dictator also embodied priorities; it was the misfortune of the Russian people that he got his priorities wrong.

Western historians have not accepted Hitler's version of his preventive war, though some, presumably influenced by the speed with which the USSR later emerged as a super-power alongside the USA, have come dangerously close to admitting the logic of Hitler's claim (similar to that used in German polemics concerning the First World War) that the Reich was threatened with encirclement. The only senior German staff officer who has taken it upon himself to defend Hitler's judgement is General Reinhard Gehlen, the post-war head of West German Intelligence. Gehlen was Halder's Adjutant until October 1940 and in April 1942 succeeded Kinzel as head of Foreign Armies East. He regards Hitler's decision as

<hr/>

[8] Texts, in German, in unpublished section of German Foreign Office archives

'correct' and indeed 'inevitable', on the grounds that
Stalin 'might have waited until 1943 or 1944, but . . .
sooner or later he was going to attack us'.[9] Paulus at
Nuremberg quoted Kinzel to the effect that 'no preparations whatever for an attack by the Soviet Union had
come to our attention'.[10] Guderian's view, after hearing
Hitler address his Commanding Officers on the eve of
the invasion, was that, 'His detailed exposition of the
reasons that led him to fight a preventive war was uncon-
vincing.'[11] Rundstedt's opinion, according to his post-
war biographer, was that 'had the Russians intended to
attack Germany, they would have done so . . . when the
entire German army was engaged . . . in the West'.[12]
Manstein, whilst admitting that Soviet strategic dispos-
itions did not indicate any immediate intention to attack,
emphasized that these 'did in fact constitute a latent
threat . . .'[13] To remove a latent threat, however is not the
same as to fight a preventive war; the invasion of Russia
was a war of aggression and no circumlocution is possible.

It remains to answer one question that must arise in
the mind of anyone who has accepted our conclusions up
to this point; if Hitler had so seriously underrated his
enemy, and if his military, economic and political planning for the campaign was so defective, how did it come
about that his venture so nearly succeeded? Part of the
answer was to be found in Germany: the Wehrmacht was
a magnificent machine, well led at all levels below the
very top and composed of battle-hardened, self-confident
soldiers, equipped with all that was requisite for the
*Blitzkrieg* that the Germans had devised and practised
since 1939 with such consummate skill. But the other
part of the answer was to be found in Russia, where
Stalin's autocracy, impatience of criticism and obsession
with ideology was as pathological as Hitler's. To docu-
ment this contention in full would require not only

[9] *The Gehlen Memoirs:* R. Gehlen (London, 1972), p.39
[10] *IMT*, VII, p.255
[11] *Panzer Leader*, op. cit., p.150
[12] *Rundstedt the Soldier*, op. cit., p.98
[13] *Lost Victories*, op. cit., p.181

another book, but access to Soviet archives on a scale comparable to the mass of the captured German documents. Instead, all we have is the thin trickle of books released in the few years following Khrushchev's de-Stalinization speech of 1956. But it is enough to substantiate one Soviet historian's forceful verdict on Stalin: 'Here was the spectacle of a leadership which professed belief in historical inevitability, which regarded itself as history's agent, trying to escape the inexorable consequences of events, to cheat history, as it were, by pitiful gestures, empty words and patent self-deception.'[14]

Stalin and the subservient ideologists whom he tolerated around him had never grasped the demonic nature of Nazism; for them the 'National-Fascists' had simply been an extreme manifestation of 'monopoly capitalism'. Marxism-Leninism taught them that capitalism, through its inner contradictions, would destroy itself; all they had to do was to watch on the side-lines and discreetly assist the mutual self-destruction of the Fascist dictators on the one hand and the Western democracies on the other. His mistake was that of seeking to prolong the conflict by helping Hitler, in the belief that, as he said in March 1939, the democracies were 'both economically and militarily . . . undoubtedly stronger than the Fascist States . . .'[15] Having committed himself to this policy in 1939, Stalin's obsession with his own infallibility would not allow him to admit that he had been mistaken. If he conceded that Germany was about to attack the USSR in 1941, then he had been wrong to join hands with Hitler in 1939 and subsequently fuel his war machine on such a massive scale. In 1965 General P. A. Kurochkin referred to Stalin's 'big blunder made before the war . . . in the evaluation of the military situation, its military and political aspects. . . . This miscalculation was primarily responsible for the unpreparedness of the Soviet armed forces . . .'[16]

[14] *Stalin and his Generals*, op. cit., p.179
[15] *DBFP, Third Series*, Vol. IV, p.412
[16] *Memoirs of a Soviet Ambassador*, op. cit., p.176

Stalin's self-justification, when he came to make it on 3 July 1941, was much the same as Neville Chamberlain's apologia for Munich: he had gained time. 'We secured to our country peace for a year and a half and the opportunity of preparing our forces.'[17] There were two misleading features of this statement. First, it implied that Hitler had been relatively passive during the same period, whereas in fact he had become immensely stronger, partly as a result of Soviet economic support. Secondly, Stalin was implying that he had made good use of the time gained. This was not the case. In spite of warnings from many sources, the invasion of June 1941 found the USSR inadequately mobilized both in the military and in the economic sense. Even if we accept Stalin's dubious argument that military mobilization would have been regarded by Hitler as provocative, nothing can justify Stalin's failure to place industry on a war footing and begin the transference of war industries from Leningrad, Moscow and Kharkov to less exposed areas. It was eventually admitted in the USSR in Stalin's own lifetime that economic planning for the third quarter of 1941 was based on the assumption that peace would continue.[18]

Stalin, in his determination to cling to the belief that Hitler would not attack him, not only ignored the reports of his own and foreign intelligence services, but rejected also the ocular evidence provided by the ever-increasing scale of Luftwaffe reconnaissance. The Red air force had begun in mid-March by bringing down a couple of intruding German aircraft; but Stalin then forbade any shooting.[19] A special squadron of Heinkels continued photography over Soviet territory, undeterred by diplomatic protests; on the day before the invasion Molotov complained to Schulenburg of no fewer than 200 violations of Soviet air space.[20] The 800 aircraft of the Red air force destroyed on the ground on the first day of the war were

[17] *Stalin:* I. Deutscher (Oxford, 1949), p.456
[18] Ibid., p.458n.
[19] *Sonderakte Barbarossa*, op. cit., p.251
[20] *Incompatible Allies*, op. cit., p.335

sacrificed to Stalin's obstinacy and pride. The Red Army fared no better; it had, as John Erickson puts it, 'some 180 minutes to prepare itself to meet the most formidable fighting machine in the world'.[21]

Stalin's timidity seems to have been based on the idea that Russia's mobilization had precipitated the First World War; but it was ill matched by a strategic emphasis on the offensive. Dumps of munitions were located close to the frontier and the troops were in forward positions ideally placed for the German tactics of deep penetration and encirclement.[22] As John Erickson points out, 'No plan for a strategic withdrawal was evident.'[23] In any case the line of fortifications on the old frontier, running south from Lake Peipus to the Dvina and Dnieper Rivers, was in process of being dismantled, 'while construction on the new frontier was proceeding at a snail's pace'.[24] As far as the Red air force was concerned, the offensive spirit was expressed in concentration on bomber production.[25]

The heavy burden of ideology had not merely prevented the exercise of normal powers of foresight; it had also gravely weakened the morale of the Soviet military machine. We discussed in Chapter VIII Stalin's purge of his armed forces, which robbed them of most of their best brains and all independence of thought; the persecutions continued until the eve of the invasion and some officers, like the future Marshal Rokossovsky, were released from detention and sent straight to the front. As one Soviet Marshal who survived has expressed it, 'At that time all aspects of our life, including the military, were too strongly influenced by the spirit of the personality cult, which fettered people's initiative, stifled their will and led to irresponsibility in some and immobility in others.'[26] In 1935 Stalin had taken a leaf out of Hitler's book by creating NKVD military units, and two years later Politi-

---

[21] *Soviet High Command*, op. cit., p.587
[22] *Stalin and his Generals*, op. cit., p.60
[23] *Soviet High Command*, op. cit., p.599
[24] *Stalin and his Generals*, op. cit., p.164
[25] Ibid., p.170
[26] Ibid., p.240

cal Commissars were given equality of status alongside Commanding Officers. This latter measure was rescinded in August 1940, but reintroduced in mid-July 1941.[27] A particularly baleful influence was exercised by Kulik, a Communist Party hatchet-man, who became Deputy Commissar for Defence. As late as January 1941 Kulik was arguing for use of the horse as against the tank; the faulty decision to break up the Tank Corps and distribute the tanks among infantry units was only reversed in March 1941.[28] When belatedly on 30 June 1941 Stalin set up a State Defence Committee of five, it included only one military man, Voroshilov, who had abundantly displayed his incapacity in the Finnish War and was about to do so again in the defence of Leningrad. The other members of the Committee, apart from Molotov, were the Party bureaucrat, Malenkov, and the sinister police chief, Beria. It was only the terrible defeats inflicted on Stalin by the Wehrmacht that forced him later in the year to delegate more authority to men of real military talent, such as Zhukov, Vassilevsky and Rokossovsky.

Inside the Soviet borders Stalin had created an ideological world that seemed to be self-contained and answerable to his will; suddenly on 22 June 1941 the realities of the world outside forced their way in. The shock at first induced something approaching a cataleptic trance; for days the dictator remained incommunicado, whilst his artificial world tumbled about his ears. As news of disaster poured in from every front, Stalin struggled to adjust himself to the situation. At last on 3 July 1941 he came to the microphone and declared the 'Great Patriotic War'. Ideology could not win the coming battles; only an appeal to save Mother Russia could serve him now. In a speech on 6 November 1941 Stalin evoked 'the manly images of our great ancestors – Alexander Nevsky, Dimitry Donsky, Kuzma Minin, Dimitry Pozharsky, Alexander Suvorov and Mikhail Kutusov . . .' Saints, Grand Princes and Tsarist Generals were summoned to the rescue of the

[27] *Soviet High Command,* op. cit., pp.553, 603
[28] *Stalin and his Generals,* op. cit., p.143

land which ideology and Stalinism had brought so close to ruin.[29] The two dictators confronted one another on the plains of Russia like two immense robots out of science fiction; gradually the stronger of the two began to gain the upper hand. When the monstrous struggle ended in Hitler's bunker in Berlin, 20 million Russian soldiers and civilians had died, the balance of power in Europe had been distorted beyond repair, and the reign of the two super-powers had begun.

[29] *Stalin,* op. cit., p.468

# BIBLIOGRAPHY

Thanks to the efforts of Prof. H. A. Jacobsen, who has edited the War Diaries of both the OKH and the OKW, we have exceptionally full accounts of what was actually said during the critical period when Hitler was making up his mind to invade the USSR. In addition, a number of his senior officers have since the war recorded their views. The problem remains one of interpreting the evidence. Whilst the soldiers had a clear interest at the post-war trials and subsequently in exculpating themselves and blaming Hitler, more reliance can be placed on the post-war testimony of Helmuth Greiner, a civilian employee (*Beamte*), who wrote the OKW War Diary from 1939 to 1943.

The historian's problem is aggravated by the fact that, although there are so many authentic accounts of what Hitler said on any given occasion, his remarks can seldom be taken at face value; each requires to be evaluated in its own context, since Hitler was always conscious of his historic role and defending it before some future court of world opinion. In addition, he had no scruples when he was seeking to persuade or browbeat his interlocutor. Two important strands of his general strategic policy, however, have been convincingly elucidated. The first is his concept of *Blitzkrieg*, which has been admirably analysed by Prof. A. S. Milward, drawing largely on Albert Speer, and by Dr B. A. Carroll, drawing largely on Gen. Georg Thomas. The second main strand is Hitler's *Stufenplan* ('step-by-step' plan), closely linked to *Blitzkrieg*, which was impressively expounded by Prof. A. Hillgruber in his '*Hitlers Strategie, Politik und Kriegsfuehrung*'. This important book is not available in English, though some of the conclusions are more briefly summarized by Prof. K. Hildebrand, whose book in English bears the title, 'The Foreign Policy of the Third Reich'. To all these books and their authors the present writer wishes to acknowledge his debt.

## GENERAL

ACKERMANN, J.: *Himmler als Ideologe* (Goettingen 1970)
ANSEL, W.: *Hitler Confronts England* (Duke, N. Carolina 1960)
ARON, R.: *Histoire de Vichy* (Paris 1954)

BELOFF, M.: *Foreign Policy of Soviet Russia* (London 1947)
BEZYMENSKY, I.: *Sonderakte Barbarossa* (Stuttgart 1968)
BIALER, I.: *Stalin and his Generals* (London 1970)
BLAU, G.: *German Campaigns in the Balkans* (Washington 1953)
BLUMENTRITT, G.: *Von Rundstedt* (London 1952)
BOBERACH, H. (Ed.): *Meldungen aus dem Reich* (Munich 1968)
BOELCKE, W. A.: *Deutschlands Ruestung im zweiten Weltkrieg* (Frankfurt 1969)
—— (Ed.): *Wollt Ihr den totalen Krieg?* (Munich 1969)
BOSL, K. (Ed.): *Das Jahr 1941 in der europaeischen Geschichte* (Munich 1972)
BRAEUTIGAM, O.: *So hat es sich Zugetragen* (Wuerzburg 1968)
BROSZAT, M.: *Nationalsozialistische Polenpolitik* (Munich 1965)
BULLOCK, A.: *Hitler: A Study in Tyranny* (London 1962)
—— (Ed.): *The Ribbentrop Memoirs* (London 1954)
BUTLER, J. R. (Ed. with GWYER, J. M.): *History of the Second World War* (London 1957)

CARR, W.: *Arms, Autarky and Aggression* (London 1972)
CARROLL, B.: *Design for Total War* (The Hague 1968)
CECIL, R.: *The Myth of the Master Race* (London 1972)
CLARK, A.: *Barbarossa* (London 1965)
COHN, N.: *Warrant for Genocide* (London 1967)
CREVELD, M. van: *Hitler's Strategy: the Balkan Clue* (Cambridge 1973)

DALLIN, A.: *German Rule in Russia* (London 1957)
DALLIN, D. J.: *Soviet Russia's Foreign Policy* (Yale 1942)
DEAKIN, F. W.: *The Case of Richard Sorge* (London 1962)
DEUTSCH, H. C.: *The Conspiracy against Hitler in the Twilight War* (Minneapolis 1968)
DEUTSCHER, I.: *Stalin* (Oxford 1949)

# Bibliography

DJILAS, M.: *Conversations with Stalin* (London 1963)

ERICKSON, J.: *The Soviet High Command* (London 1962)

FABRY, P. W.: *Der Hitler-Stalin Pakt* (Darmstadt 1962)
FREUND, G.: *The Unholy Alliance* (London 1957)

GEHLEN, R.: *The Gehlen Memoirs* (London 1972)
GENOUD, F. (Ed.): *The Testament of Hitler* (London 1961)
GIBSON, H. (Ed.): *The Hassell Diaries* (London 1948)
GILBERT, F.: *Hitler Directs His War* (Oxford 1950)
GOERLITZ, W.: *The German General Staff* (London 1953)
—— *Keitel Verbrecher oder Offizier?* (Frankfurt 1961)
GORBATOV, A. V.: *Years Off My Life* (London 1964)
GREINER, H.: *Die oberste Wehrmachtfuehrung* (Wiesbaden 1951)
GUDERIAN, H.: *Panzer Leader* (London 1952)
GWYER, J. M.: *see* BUTLER, J. R.

HAERTLE, H. (Ed.): *Grossdeutschland; Traum und Tragoedie* (Munich 1970)
HALDER, F.: *Hitler as War Lord* (London 1950)
HEIBER, H. (Ed.): *Lagebesprechungen im Fuehrer Haupquartier* (Munich 1963)
HEIM, F. (with PHILIPPI, A.): *Feldzug gegen Sowjetrussland* (Stuttgart 1962)
HILDEBRAND, K.: *The Foreign Policy of the Third Reich* (London 1973)
HILGER, G. (with MEYER, A.): *Incompatible Allies* (New York 1953)
HILLGRUBER, A.: *Deutschlands Rolle in der Vorgeschichte der beiden Weltkriege* (Goettingen 1967)
—— *Hitlers Strategie, Politik und Kriegsfuehrung* (Frankfurt 1968)
—— (Ed.): *Staatsmaenner und Diplomaten bei Hitler* (Frankfurt 1967)
—— (Ed.): *Hitlers Tischgespraeche im Fuehrer Hauptquartier* (Munich 1968)
HINGLEY, R.: *J. Stalin: Man and Legend* (London 1974)
HINSLEY, F.: *Hitler's Strategy* (Cambridge 1951)
HOEHNE, H.: *The Order of the Death's Head* (London 1969)
HUBATSCH, W.: *Hitlers Weisungen fuer die Kriegsfuehrung* (Munich 1965)

ILNYTZKJ, R.: *Deutschland und die Ukraine* (Munich 1958)

JACOBSEN, H. A.: *Nationalsozialistische Aussenpolitik* (Frankfurt 1968)
—— (Ed.): *Der zweite Weltkrieg in Chronik und Dokumenten* (Darmstadt 1962)
—— *Kriegstagebuch des* OKW, Vol. I. (Frankfurt 1961)
—— *Halder; Kriegstagebuch* (Stuttgart 1963)
JAECKEL, E.: *Hitlers Weltanschauung* (Tuebingen 1969)

KEMPNER, R. M.: *Das dritte Reich im Kreuzverhoer* (Munich 1969)
KENNAN, G.: *Soviet Foreign Policy* (New York 1960)
KESSELRING, A.: *Memoirs* (London 1953)
KLEIN, B.: *Germany's Economic Preparations for War* (Cambridge, Mass. 1959)
KLEIST, P.: *European Tragedy* (London 1965)
KOCHAN, L.: *The Struggle for Germany* (Edinburgh 1963)
KOEHL, R. L.: *RKFDV; German Resettlement Policy* (Harvard 1957)
KORDT, E.: *Wahn und Wirklichkeit* (Stuttgart 1948)

LAQUEUR, W.: *Russia and Germany* (London 1965)
LEACH, B. A.: *German Strategy against Russia* (Oxford 1973)
LEVERKUEHN, P.: *German Military Intelligence* (London 1954)
LIDDELL HART, B. H.: *On the Other Side of the Hill* (London 1951)
LUNDIN, L.: *Finland in the Second World War* (Indiana 1957)
LUPKE, H.: *Japans Russlandpolitik* (Frankfurt 1962)

MANSTEIN, E. von: *Lost Victories* (Chicago 1958)
MARKERT, W. (Ed.): *Deutsch-Russiache Beziehungen von Bismarck bis zur Gegenwart* (Stuttgart 1964)
MEYER, A.: *see* HILGER, G.
MEYER, H. C.: *Mitteleuropa* (The Hague 1955)
MILWARD, A. S.: *The German Economy at War* (London 1965)
MUELLER-HILLEBRAND, B.: *Das Heer* (Frankfurt 1956)

O'NEILL, R. J.: *The German Army and the Nazi Party* (London 1966)

ORLOW, D.: *The Nazis in the Balkans* (Pittsburgh 1968)

PHILIPPI, A.: *see* HEIM, F.

PIETROWSKI, S. (Ed.): *Hans Frank's Diary* (Warsaw 1961)

PRESSEISEN, E. L.: *Germany and Japan* (The Hague 1958)

RAUSCHNING, H.: *Hitler Speaks* (London 1939)

—— *Germany's Revolution of Destruction* (London 1939)

REITLINGER, G.: *SS-Alibi of a Nation* (London 1950)

—— *House Built on Sand* (London 1960)

RICH, N.: *Hitler's War Aims* (London 1973)

ROBERTSON, E. M.: *Hitler's Pre-war Policy and Military Plans* (London 1963)

ROSENBERG, A.: *Der Zukunft einer deutschen Aussenpolitik* (Munich 1927)

ROSSI, A.: *The Russo-German Alliance* (London 1950)

SALISBURY, H. E. (Ed.): *Zhukov's Greatest Battles* (London 1969)

SCHELLENBERG, W.: *The Labyrinth* (New York 1956)

SCHRAMM, P. E.: *Hitler: Man and Military Leader* (London 1972)

SCHREIBER, H.: *Teuton and Slav* (London 1965)

SCHWEITZER, A.: *Big Business in the Third Reich* (London 1964)

SEATON, A.: *The Russo-German War* (London 1971)

SERAPHIM, H. G. (Ed.): *Das politische Tagebuch Rosenbergs* (Munich 1964)

SHIRER, W. L.: *Berlin Diary* (London 1941)

SPEER, A.: *Inside the Third Reich* (London 1970)

STEIN, G. H.: *The Waffen SS* (London 1966)

STRIK-STRIKFELDT, W.: *Gegen Hitler und Stalin* (Mainz 1970)

TAYLOR, T. (Ed.): *Hitler's Secret Book* (New York 1961)

TELPUKHOVSKY, B. S.: *Die Sowjetische Geschichte des grossen vaterlaendischen Krieges* (Frankfurt 1961)

THOMAS, G.: *Geschichte der Wehrwirtschaft* (Boppard 1966)

TREVOR ROPER, H. (Ed.): *Hitler's War Directives* (London 1964)

—— *Hitler's Table Talk* (London 1953)

UPTON, A. F.: *Finland in Crisis* (London 1964)

WARLIMONT, W.: *Inside Hitler's HQ* (London 1964)
WARNER, G.: *Pierre Laval* (London 1968)
WEINBERG, G. L.: *Germany and the Soviet Union* (Leyden 1954)
WEIZSAECKER, E. von: *Memoirs* (London 1951)
WERTH, A.: *Russia at War* (London 1964)
WHEATLEY, R.: *Operation Sea Lion* (Oxford 1958)
WHEELER BENNETT, J.: *Brest-Litovsk: The Forgotten Peace* (New York 1939)
—— *The Nemesis of Power* (London 1953)
WISKEMANN, E.: *Germany's Eastern Neighbours* (Oxford 1956)
WOODWARD, E. L.: *British Foreign Policy in the Second World War* (London 1962)

## DOCUMENT COLLECTIONS

BAYNES, N. (Ed.): *Hitler's Speeches* (Oxford 1942)
DEGRAS, J. (Ed.): *Calendar of Soviet Documents* (London 1948)
DOMARUS, M. (Ed.): *Hitler, Reden und Proklamationen* (Wuerzburg 1962)
HMSO: *Documents on British Foreign Policy*, Third Series (London 1950–3)
—— *Documents on German Foreign Policy*, Series D (London 1953–6)
HOFER, W. (Ed.): *Der Nationalsozialismus, Dokumente* (Frankfurt 1957)
INTERNATIONAL MILITARY TRIBUNAL, *Trial of the Major War Criminals* (Nuremberg 1947)
TOYNBEE, A. (Ed.): *Documents on International Affairs* (Oxford 1954)

## UNPUBLISHED DOCUMENTS

ROBERTSON, E. M.: Monograph on Barbarossa (March 1952)
SPEER, A.: Commentary on W. A. Boelcke's Deutschlands Ruestung im zweiten Weltkrieg (December 1969)

# Bibliography
## ARTICLES etc.

BOCIURKIW, B. R.: 'Soviet Nationalities Policy' (*World Today* 1974)

CREVELD, M. van: 'War Lord Hitler' (*European Studies Review* 1974)

ERICKSON, J.: 'Panslavism' (*Historical Association* 1964)

HEIBER, H.: 'Der Generalplan Ost' (*Vierteljahreshefte fuer Zeitgeschichte* 1958)

HENKE, J.: 'Hitler und England' (*VfZg* 1973)

HILLGRUBER, A. (with SERAPHIM, H. G.): 'Hitlers Entschluss zum Angriff auf Russland' (*VfZg* 1954)

—— 'Japan und der Fall Barbarossa' (*Wehrwissenschaftliche Rundschau* 1968)

—— 'Die Endloesung und das Ostimperium' (*VfZg* 1972)

KEMPNER, R. M.: 'Rosenberg's Diary' (*Der Monat* 1949)

KLUKE, P.: 'Nationalsozialistische Europaideologie' (*VfZg* 1955)

LANGE, K.: 'Der terminus Lebensraum in *Mein Kampf*' (*VfZg* 1965)

PRESSEISEN, E. L.: 'Prelude to Barbarossa' (*Journal of Modern History* 1960)

RIEDEL, M.: 'Bergbau usw. in der Ukraine' (*VfZg* 1973)

ROPP, W. DE: 'I Spied on Hitler' (*Daily Mail* Oct.-Nov. 1957)

SCHULZE, H.: 'Der Oststaat-Plan 1919' (*VfZg* 1970)

SPEIDEL, H.: 'Reichswehr und Rote Armee' (*VfZg* 1953)

STRANG, LORD: 'The Moscow Negotiations' (*Leeds University Press* 1968)

VOGELSANG, T.: 'Hitlers Brief an Reichenau' (*VfZg* 1959)

WEINBERG, G. L.: 'Der deutsche Entschluss zum Angriff auf die SU' (*VfZg* 1953)

# INDEX